Mastering

Samsung Galaxy

S24 Series

Comprehensive Guide on Everything You Need
to Know to Master Your New Samsung Galaxy
S24, S24 Plus and S24 Ultra

TABLE OF CONTENTS

INTRODUCING THE S24 SERIES

With the launch of the new Galaxy S24 Ultra, Galaxy S24+, and Galaxy S24, Samsung Electronics unleashed new mobile experiences powered by Galaxy AI. The Galaxy S series ushers in a new era that will permanently alter how mobile devices enable their users. With the Galaxy S24 series, artificial intelligence (AI) enhances almost every aspect of the user experience. It allows for barrier-free communication through intelligent text and call translations, maximizes creative freedom through Galaxy's ProVisual Engine, and sets a new standard for search that will transform how Galaxy users explore their surroundings. The Galaxy S24 series sparks the next ten years of mobile innovation and revolutionizes how people connect with the outside world. "Galaxy AI is based on a rich history of innovation and a thorough comprehension of mobile user behavior. Galaxy AI will enable people all over the world to take new opportunities in their daily lives.

Let's take a look at the amazing features embedded in this wonderful series;

A Delight Everyday

With its introduction of meaningful intelligence, Galaxy AI seeks to improve all aspects of life, particularly communication, which is the phone's primary function. The Galaxy S24 makes it simpler than ever to overcome language barriers when necessary. You can converse with a foreign student or coworker and make a reservation while on vacation abroad. Through Live Translate, two-way, real-time phone call translations (both text and voice) within the native app are possible. Conversations remain private thanks to on-device AI, and no third-party apps are needed. People positioned across from one another can read a text transcription of each other's remarks by using an Interpreter to translate live conversations instantly on a split screen. It even functions without Wi-Fi or cellular data. Chat Assist can assist in fine-tuning conversational tones for messages and other apps so that communication sounds as intended, such as a courteous message to a colleague or a succinct and memorable statement for a social media caption. The Samsung Keyboard's three AI systems can translate messages into thirteen different languages in real time. Android Auto enables you to stay connected while maintaining your attention on the road by automatically summarizing incoming messages and suggesting pertinent responses and actions, such as sending someone your ETA.

With Note Assist in Samsung Notes, which offers AI-generated summaries, template creation that simplifies notes with pre-made formats, and cover creation that renders notes easy to spot with a brief preview, organization is also greatly enhanced. Transcript Assist employs artificial intelligence (AI) and speech-to-text technology to transcribe, summarize, and even translate voice recordings featuring multiple speakers. The Galaxy S24 series expands upon the core advantages of the phone beyond communication.

Almost every aspect of life has changed as a result of online searches. The Galaxy S24 is the first phone to introduce Google's intuitive, gesture-driven Circle to Search, making it a significant milestone in the history of search. With just a gesture, Galaxy opened up new avenues of discovery for its users by collaborating with Google, the global leader in search, to provide them with an amazing new tool. Users can circle, highlight, annotate, or tap anything on the Galaxy S24's screen to see beneficial, high-quality search results by long pressing the home button. When a friend posts a picture of a stunning landmark on social media or discovers a surprising fun fact on YouTube Shorts, it can quickly lead to an accurate search to find out more without requiring them to leave the app. Additionally, generative AI-powered overviews for specific searches can offer useful context and information gathered from across the web, and users can ask more in-depth and sophisticated questions based on their location. It is that simple.

Provisual Engine

The ProVisual Engine9 of the Galaxy S24 series is a full suite of AI-powered tools that optimizes creative freedom and revolutionizes image capture capabilities from setup to social media sharing. The blurry, pixelated photos from long ago are long gone. With its new 5x optical zoom lens, the Quad Tele System of the Galaxy S24 Ultra combines with the 50MP sensor to provide optical-quality performance at zoom levels ranging from 2x, 3x, 5x, and 10 x 10 magnification, all made possible by the Adaptive Pixel Sensor. Images with improved digital zoom also display incredibly clear results at 100x.

Upgraded Nigtography

Even at a high magnification, images and videos captured with the Galaxy S24 Space Zoom's enhanced Nightography feature look amazing. The larger 1.4 μm pixel size on the Galaxy S24 ultra—60% bigger than the previous model—allows you to capture more light in low light. With larger optical image stabilizer (OIS) angles and improved hand-shake compensation, the Galaxy S24 Ultra has less blur. Both the front and rear cameras have dedicated ISP blocks for noise reduction when filming and the Galaxy S24 uses gyro information analysis to discern between the subject's and the filmmaker's movements. This makes it possible to reduce noise in videos even at great distances and to see them clearly in the dark.

Innovative Galaxy AI editing tools allow for basic edits like erasure, re-compose, and remaster after fantastic shots are taken. Edit Suggestion uses Galaxy AI to make precisely the right adjustments and suggestions for every photo, making optimizations simpler and more effective. Generative Edit can use generative AI to fill in portions of an image's background, giving users even more artistic freedom and control. Artificial Intelligence will fill in the borders of an uneven image. AI allows users to modify the subject's position and creates a flawlessly blended background in the original location when an object needs to be moved slightly to be in the ideal spot. When Galaxy S24 uses generative AI to enhance a picture, a watermark will show up in the image's metadata. Additionally, the new Instant Slow-mo feature can create extra frames based on actions to smoothly slow down action-packed occasions for a closer look if a fast-paced video needs to be slowed down.

Premium Performance

AI is becoming more and more integrated into daily life, and performance power needs to keep up with the demands. Playing games. intensive video editing and recording. Planning a trip by hopping between five different apps. The Galaxy S24's improved chipset, 15-inch display, and other features make it an amazing experience no matter what the task at hand. Galaxy S24 Ultra devices are all outfitted with the Snapdragon® 8 Gen 3 Mobile Platform.16 With remarkable NPU improvement; this chipset is specially optimized for Galaxy users to process AI incredibly efficiently. Moreover, 1-120 Hz adaptive refresh rates increase performance efficiency in all three Galaxy S24 models. Thanks to advancements in both hardware and software, gaming on the Galaxy is more potent. With a 1.9-fold larger vapor chamber, the Galaxy S24 Ultra has an ideal thermal control system that maximizes sustained performance power and improves device surface temperature. Realistic images with excellent shadow and reflection effects are made possible by ray tracing. Additionally, the Galaxy S24 allowed users to experience more optimized versions of well-known international mobile games thanks to partnerships with top gaming companies.

Design improvements with fewer and more balanced bezels throughout the Galaxy S24 series allow for larger screen sizes on the 6.7-inch and 6.2-inch screens of the Galaxy S24+ and Galaxy S24 within almost the same dimensions, making it simpler to fully immerse yourself in any viewing experience. The 6.8-inch flatter display on the Galaxy S24 Ultra is designed for both productivity and viewing. Additionally, the Galaxy S24+ now supports QHD+ at the same level as the Galaxy S24 Ultra.

Advanced Security

The defense-grade, multi-layer security platform Samsung Knox, which is integrated into the Galaxy S24, guards sensitive data and wards off threats with real-time threat detection, end-to-end secure hardware, and collaborative protection. In the age of artificial intelligence, Samsung is still dedicated to giving customers choice and control over their devices. With the Advanced Intelligence settings on the Galaxy S24, users can completely control how much of their data is used to improve AI experiences. This includes the ability to stop data from being processed online for AI features. Passkeys also advance the Knox Matrix22 vision of a passwordless, connected, and secure future. By providing digital credentials for easy and safe access to a user's registered websites and applications on all of their trusted devices, passkeys aid in thwarting phishing attacks. When users backup, sync, or restore their data with Samsung Cloud, Enhanced Data Protection provides end-to-end encryption. This feature enables Galaxy S24 users to connect to other devices while maintaining sync and security.

Passkeys also advance the Knox Matrix22 vision of a passwordless, connected, and secure future. By providing digital credentials for easy and safe access to a user's registered websites and applications on all of their trusted devices, passkeys aid in thwarting phishing attacks. When users backup, sync, or restore their data with Samsung Cloud, Enhanced Data Protection provides end-to-end encryption. This feature enables Galaxy S24 users to connect to other devices while maintaining sync and security. This guarantees that, even if a server is compromised or account credentials are stolen, the data can only be encrypted or decrypted on the user's devices, meaning that only the user can view it. Additionally, a recovery code can help stop data loss if access to a trusted device is lost. Samsung's long list of cutting-edge security and privacy features, which includes Knox Vault, Security & Privacy Dashboard, Auto Blocker, Secure Wi-Fi, Private Share, Maintenance Mode, and more, safeguards the Galaxy S24 as well.

OVERVIEW OF THIS BOOK

This incredible guidebook has been meticulously crafted to assist you in working your way through the mind-blowing S24 series. You will have the opportunity to discover all about the numerous new features that Samsung has included in its most recent product release by reading this book. This book contains a wealth of information, including instructions on how to set up a Samsung account, information on maintaining physical fitness and health, and details on the many applications to which you have access and may put to use with products in the S24 series. The following are excerpts that can be found in each chapter of this incredible book; as you read along, make sure that you have your phone close at hand so that you can easily put what you learn into practice. This book also has some activities for you at the end of each chapter so you can test your knowledge about all you have read in each chapter.

CHAPTER 1: SETTINGS UP SAMSUNG GALAXY S24, S24 PLUS, AND S24 ULTRA

In the first chapter of this book, you will learn how to set up your device, which might be an S24, an S24 Plus, or an S24 Ultra, depending on the model you have. This after you must have read a welcome note by the author of this book, giving great tips and insights about what you are to expect from this amazing book. You will also gain an understanding of the many add-ons and accessories that are compatible with your smartphone, such as the Pen and a Samsung wristwatch, amongst others. You will gain more insight on how to set up your device especially if this is the first time you are making use of a Samsung product and you have a need to bring your data from the previous phone you are using be it an Android or even an iPhone. This book will guide you into transferring all of your documents seamlessly and also help you set up a Samsung account. Lastly, there is a special guide in the first chapter of this book which is about the tips you must take into consideration if you want to maximize the use of the phone and also ensure you are not trying to get a technician to check it for you in just a few months from purchase.

Chapter 2: Navigating Around the Samsung S24 Series

You are now prepared to utilize your gadget appropriately. You will have no trouble navigating the phone after reading this chapter. You will be instructed on how to manage the touch screen, as well as learn about the home screen and app drawer so that you can get the most out of your device. You will also learn how to personalize the home screen so that it appears exactly the way you want it to appear. This includes customizing the app icons, wallpaper, widgets, and quick settings, among other things. In the end, you will also discover more about the Edge Panel, including what it is and how you can make the most of using it. You will also find your way into the notification panel in this chapter where you will get to learn about controlling the media playback and also controlling other devices that might be close to you. Furthermore in this chapter, you will get to learn about the use of screen capture and screen recording which are amazing features used in getting a snap of pictures you might find fascinating on the internet. Lastly, you will get to learn about the use of the keyboard which includes how to enter text with the use of the keyboard button and also how you can copy and paste text from one place in the phone to another if you want to avoid the use of the keyboard. You will also learn about extracting text which is the feature that concludes this chapter!

Chapter 3: Transfer Content with Samsung Smart Switch

You are going to get an introduction to the Samsung Smart Switch, which is a tool that can be used to move content from one location to another. You will understand how to create a wireless transfer, and you will also learn how to import content from iCloud, so going from an iPhone to a Samsung device won't be an issue for you. You will also learn how to move data by employing a USB cable, a MicroSD card, or a USB flash drive. Also, you will learn how to transfer data from a Windows phone in addition to transferring data from a PC.

Chapter 4: Phone

This chapter is an essential component of the reason you purchased the phone in the first place, so make sure you read it! In this section, you will understand how to make phone calls, answer incoming calls, and decline a call. You will also gain knowledge on how to block a number, which will prevent any calls or text messages from being received from that particular number in the future. You will have no trouble with adding a new contact, and you'll also be able to check and customize your voicemail settings once you are through reading this chapter. The call assist is another feature that you will get to learn about in this chapter. This feature assists in giving a response to the other person on the phone and can be quite useful when you are engaged with some other things and at the same time want to engage in a meaningful conversation with someone over the phone. The live translate feature is another amazing addition that you will also get to learn about in this chapter. With the use of your S24, you can now translate your language to another. Doing business with foreign partners who don't speak the same language as you do is now much easier as you will not need to get a translator since you already have one in your unique S24.

Chapter 5: Contacts App

Another essential component of the phone is going to be dissected in this chapter. You will learn how to create contacts, edit contacts that you have already created, and add contacts to favorites or groups. You will also learn about the creation of groups which could either be family or friends in school or at work. Having this group is quite important as it helps to save time when there is a need to communicate with a group of people especially if it's the same message you want to pass across. Lastly, you will also learn how to merge duplicate contacts. This comes in handy if you have a contact with two different phone numbers, you can merge such with ease making your contact list much more organized.

Chapter 6: Messages

This chapter will focus exclusively on the messaging application. In this chapter, you will discover how to send messages, check them, sort them, delete them, and forward them. You will also learn about the SOS message and exactly how to send an SOS message.

Chapter 7: Settings

This section will teach you the ins and outs of the device's configuration menu. You'll learn how to access your phone's settings, make full use of its display options, and switch between different displays modes. In this chapter, you will also learn about the use of motion smoothness, lock screen, AOD, extend lock, always display as well as the use of the internet.

Chapter 8: Sound, Vibration, and Notification Settings

You are going to learn everything there is to know about sounds, vibrations, and notifications in this chapter. You will also learn how to adjust the equalizer and customize the ringtone, as well as how to regulate the volume. The ringtone configuration includes selecting the tone that best suits your taste. You will learn about the "do not disturb" option for the notifications, as well as how to change the settings for the notifications that appear on the lock screen. You will also acquire knowledge on the one-of-a-kind setting of Dolby Atmos.

Chapter 9: Connection Settings

It is always necessary for you to connect your phone to either another phone or any other device that is enabled with Wi-Fi or Bluetooth. In this chapter, you will learn about a variety of modes of connection, such as via Wi-Fi and Bluetooth. You will also learn about Near Field Communication (NFC) technology. You will also learn how to use your phone to make payments, as well as how to use airplane mode, mobile networks, mobile hotspots, and other settings for various types of connections.

Chapter 10: Lock Screen and Security

It does not make a difference if you are negligent or not; losing your phone is something that may happen to everyone. In this chapter, you will learn about the different ways in which you may keep your phone safe. You will become familiar with the many types of screen locks, such that after you have used one of them, no one will be capable of taking control of your phone without first obtaining your authorization. This chapter will continue discussing the numerous choices available for ensuring safety. This chapter will teach you how to utilize the tool "find my mobile," which can assist you in locating your phone if it is misplaced or stolen. In addition to that, you will get knowledge on the application of biometrics, such as face recognition and fingerprint recognition. You will also learn about digital well-being, as well as how to set up parental controls so that you will be prepared to do so if you buy this device for one of your children and want to ensure their safety online. Ultimately, you will also be provided with all the information necessary regarding Samsung Pass.

Chapter 11: Your Apps

You will become familiar with the many applications that are at your disposal for use within this device by reading through this chapter. The applications that are being discussed are organized into three sections; Samsung, Google, and Microsoft respectively. Furthermore, you will learn how to get new applications downloaded if the app you would like to make use of cannot be found in Google Apps or the Samsung store. Also, you will learn about the best free applications you can download to ensure that you enjoy your phone even more and get the best out of it.

Chapter 12: Using the Camera

Since nearly everyone enjoys being behind the lens of a camera, there is a lot of excitement surrounding this particular piece of equipment. In this chapter, you will learn about the camera, which will include the many different methods that the camera may be started with, as well as the many different shooting modes that are accessible in the camera of your device. You will also learn how to create an album, the many ways in which you may save your photographs and videos, as well as how to save both your images and videos on OneDrive. You will also learn about creating an album from the pictures or videos you must have taken. You will get to learn about various video modes and how to get the best settings out of your camera.

Chapter 13: Gallery

In this chapter, you will learn everything you require to know about the Gallery. You will learn how to access the gallery app, view the photographs that are stored within the app, and also how to edit the pictures that are stored inside the app at this point. You will also learn how to take screenshots and record your screen, as well as how to play videos, share photographs and videos, and collaborate on creating content.

Chapter 14: The Calendar and Clock Apps

You will learn pretty much everything you need to know about the Calendar after reading this chapter. In this chapter, you will learn how to add events to your calendar, how to delete or update existing events, and how to link your calendar to other accounts.

Chapter 15: Samsung DeX

In this chapter, you will go through the Samsung Dex in great detail. You will discover how to make use of it, as well as how you can efficiently obtain control of it.

Chapter 16: Samsung Wallet (Samsung Pay)

Do you know that you can use your Samsung phone to make payments? If not, you should look into it right away by ensuring you read this chapter thoroughly. This chapter will provide an in-depth discussion on the specifics of how this can be accomplished by guiding you through the use of Samsung Wallet.

Chapter 17: How to Edit Videos with the InShot App

In this chapter, everything you need to know about editing videos using InShot is covered in detail. You will learn how to import photographs and videos, how to order clips, how to delete clips, how to resize videos, how to create a transition, how to freeze videos, and how to save videos, along with a great deal of other information regarding the InShot application.

Chapter 18: Samsung Notes and Advanced Features

This chapter focuses on a comprehensive discussion of Samsung's Notes. In this section, you will acquire knowledge on how to make use of both the notes app and the S Pen. In addition to this, you will gain an understanding of the myriad of capabilities offered by the S Pen. You will also learn about the use of motions and gestures, Bixby, and other tips and tricks that can make you enjoy your device even more.

Chapter 19: Samsung Health

Samsung isn't just concerned that you purchase their phone and that the company makes a profit from the purchase. They are also worried about how you are doing physically. This chapter provides an in-depth discussion of Samsung Health.

Chapter 20: Make a Call with Google Duo

This chapter covers all you need to know about using Google Duo, including how to make calls, initiate a group call, create a group, change the name of a group, and even make calls using Google Duo from another application.

Chapter 21: Troubleshooting Tips

The fact that this is a new phone doesn't mean there may not be certain lags. This chapter explains the few lags you might experience when you are making use of this phone and provides solutions to those problems so you always have your lovely phone in perfect condition. Now that the excerpts included in each of the chapters have been covered, let's go on to discuss the book in greater depth.

CHAPTER 1

SETTING UP SAMSUNG GALAXY S24, GALAXY S24 PLUS, GALAXY S24 ULTRA

Personal Note from the Author

With great care and attention to detail, this book has been created to give you the best assistance possible when navigating through the devices that are part of the recently released S24. Go over each chapter in detail, making sure to pay close attention to any instructions about this device and its security.

Features of Samsung Galaxy S24, Galaxy S24 Plus, and Galaxy S24 Ultra

In this section, you will learn about the major difference that exists between each of the Galaxy S24 series.

Design

The standard Galaxy S24 and S24 Plus models share the same aluminum frame and design as their S24 counterparts. They still provide IP68 water and dust resistance for increased durability, just like the S24 Ultra. In addition, all of the phones are once more offered in black, purple, and yellow; however, the green color way of the S24 lineup has been replaced with gray. The S24 and S24 Plus weigh 5.89 ounces (167 grams) and 12.25 ounces (196 grams), respectively, less than the Ultra but lacking the built-in S Pen stylus. The S24 Ultra, weighing 8.22 ounces (232 grams), is the heaviest model in the lineup. This is partially due to its new titanium frame, which is reminiscent of the iPhone 15 Pro and adds weight while also potentially improving durability. Additionally, the S24 Ultra removes the curved edges of its predecessor in favor of a flat screen, which should facilitate writing with the S Pen. Additionally, unlike the S24 and S24 Plus, which have Corning Gorilla Glass Victus 2 cover glass, it is protected by Corning Gorilla Armor. Samsung says the Corning Gorilla Armor is the most scratch-resistant Gorilla Glass yet, and it should reduce reflections by up to 75%.

Storage and RAM options

The S24 has two storage and memory options: 256GB and 512GB, each with 8GB of RAM. The Galaxy S24 Plus keeps the same 256GB and 512GB storage options but sports 12GB of RAM instead of 8GB like its predecessor. In the meantime, the S24 Ultra keeps offering 256GB, 512GB, and 1TB of storage space in addition to 12GB of RAM.

Display

All of the Galaxy S24 models still have OLED screens, but they differ slightly in size from model to model this time around. The Galaxy S24 Plus boasts a 6.7-inch screen, while the standard S24 has a 6.2-inch screen. Both models are 0.1 inches larger than their S24 equivalents. With 6.8 inches, the Galaxy S24 Ultra is still the biggest. The S24 series is not only larger but also brighter, with peak brightness levels reaching 2,600 nits. High-resolution 1440p screens are another feature shared by the Plus and the Ultra that improves upon the S24 Plus. The S24, however, is limited to a 1080p screen. Gamers will be pleased to hear that each game still offers a maximum refresh rate of 120Hz. More engaging graphics and fluid scrolling are made possible by this. The S24 Ultra offers the largest vapor chamber cooling system available, nearly twice the size of the S24 Ultra's. The S24 series also features larger vapor chamber cooling systems than their predecessors. This means that it should continue to operate at its best for longer periods and avoid overheating during extended gaming sessions.

AI Features

Numerous native AI-powered tools, all based on Google's Gemini foundational models, are included with the new S24 lineup. By the middle of 2024, these AI features will also be available for the Z Flip 5, Z Fold 5, and S24 lineup. One of the new features is Circle to Search, which lets you search Google without having to switch between apps for anything you circle. We didn't have much time to experiment with the feature, but we found it to be pretty helpful. It was successful as well; for example, we were unable to fool it into thinking that a fake plant was the real thing. Additionally, Samsung unveiled several new tools for communication, such as Live Translate, which can translate text messages and two-way calls into thirteen different languages in real time. With the help of Transcript Assist, you can translate, summarize, and transcribe audio files. Additionally, "tone tweak" offers text suggestions to help you make your writing sound more formal or informal. The Notes Assist feature, which immediately formats and sums up your notes with bullet points, is another noteworthy writing feature. To free your mind to concentrate on driving, Android Auto summarizes incoming messages and provides voice command suggestions for replies.

Software update policy and Android 14

When you purchase any of Samsung's new Galaxy S24 phones, the company also promises seven generations of OS upgrades and seven years of security updates. That corresponds with Google's Pixel 8 lineup's support period. Additionally, it is superior to the S24's, which receives five years' worth of security updates in addition to four generations of Android version updates. The new S24 series is powered by Android 14, just like Google's Pixel 8 series and the S24 lineup. This implies that you can benefit from features like lock screen customization. Additionally, you can use your phone as a webcam and use your fingerprint to log into third-party apps.

Cameras

Regarding camera specifications, the S24 and S24 Plus are identical to their predecessors. Their triple camera array consists of a 12-megapixel selfie camera, a 10-megapixel telephoto with 3x optical zoom, a 12-megapixel ultrawide, and a 50-megapixel main camera. With an improved 50MP 5x telephoto and a 200-megapixel primary camera, the S24 Ultra provides the most powerful setup available. It has a 12-megapixel ultrawide and a 10-megapixel 3x telephotos in addition to a 12-megapixel front camera, just like the S24 and S24 Plus.

Processing Power

A newly developed, customized version of Qualcomm's Snapdragon 8 Gen 3 for Samsung phones powers all three of the phones in the US. While enhancing performance, the new Snapdragon 8 Gen 3 chipset powers the generative AI features on the device. Additionally, the chipset enables improved ray tracing, giving game light reflections a more realistic appearance. Only the S24 and S24 Plus with an Exynos chipset are available for purchase if you are not a US citizen. According to Samsung, this shouldn't have an impact on how well the on-device AI functions. However, the Snapdragon 8 Gen 3 is included with the S24 Ultra regardless of where you purchase it.

Batteries and Charging

With a 4,000mAh capacity, the S24 has the smallest battery, while the S24 Ultra has the largest, at 5,000mAh. The S24 Ultra has a battery life of the same, easily lasting a full day. With 4,900mAh, the S24 Plus's battery capacity this year is almost identical to that of the Ultra. It might last almost as long as the Ultra. All of the phones can also be charged wirelessly, however, there is a catch: they only support Qi wireless charging, not the faster, more recent Qi2, which is similar to MagSafe. With a 45W adapter, Samsung claims the S24 Ultra and S24 Plus can reach 65 percent charge in about 30 minutes when charging via wire. With a 25W adapter, the S24 can charge to 50% capacity in the same amount of time.

Accessories for Your Device

With an abundance of remarkable features and significant advancements, the Galaxy S24 series is poised to completely transform the smartphone landscape. Nevertheless, making the appropriate accessory purchases is essential if you want to fully customize and optimize your user experience. This section will cover a variety of necessary add-ons that will improve the functionality of your Samsung Galaxy S24 while also giving it a stylish touch.

Samsung Galaxy S24 Case: Slim yet Strong

A sturdy case is an essential piece of gear because your priceless Galaxy S24 deserves the best defense possible against dings and scratches. Made from the finest aramid fiber frequently used in the aerospace and military industries, PITAKA's MagEZ Case 4 offers remarkable strength without sacrificing weight. You can be confident that wear and tear won't affect your device. In addition, the chemical stability of the case gives it remarkable resistance against yellowing over time.

You may be concerned that a robust phone case will have an ugly and bulky design. But that's not at all what PITAKA's Galaxy S24 phone case is. With a weight of only 18.6g (min) and a thickness of only 1.0mm (min), this case makes sure that your device's sleekness is always on show. The S24 case also goes one step further, showcasing a 3D textured pattern made possible by unique painting and processing. This pattern not only gives the case more aesthetic appeal but also provides an anti-slip grip that lessens the possibility of unintentional drops.

Samsung Galaxy S24 Screen Protector: Ultrathin and Clear

The screen protector is an essential piece of equipment to keep your device's screen in perfect condition. With an impressive 7H hardness rating, PITAKA's S24 screen protector effectively guards against scratches and dirt. With its thin 0.28mm thickness, the screen protector for the Galaxy S24 guarantees accurate touch sensitivity and prompt response to your on-screen fingerprint authentication.

Because of its high transparency, your device's display maintains its HD clarity and brilliant colors, giving you an immersive visual experience that's similar to seeing a naked screen. In addition, the screen is seamlessly covered by the 2.5D curved edge design, which facilitates fluid page swiping. Notably, the screen protector ensures a bubble-free and simple installation process by perfectly lining up with the majority of Galaxy S24 cases.

Samsung Galaxy S24 Wireless Charger: Hands-free and convenient

Wireless chargers surpass convenience in terms of charging, even though fast chargers and fast charging cables improve the charging experience. The 3-in-1 MagEZ Slider 2 from PITAKA is a Qi-enabled earbud, Apple Watch, and Galaxy S24 compatible wireless charging station. With a MagSafe case on, you can easily snap your S24 onto the wireless charger for up to 7.5W of wireless charging because of its powerful magnetic force. Moreover, this MagSafe wireless charger allows you to mount your phone in either portrait or landscape orientation, which makes watching videos hands-free possible. You can effortlessly access your phone from any angle thanks to its 360-degree rotation feature.

Samsung Galaxy S24 Car Phone Holder: Stable and Secure

For those who are always on the go, a dependable car phone mount is a necessary addition to your Galaxy S24 gear. The MagEZ Car Mount Pro 2 from PITAKA steps in to provide a safe and practical solution. This MagSafe phone holder makes sure that your S24, which is fitted with a MagSafe case, stays in place even on the bumpiest roads thanks to its powerful magnetic force. Your phone will stay charged the entire way thanks to the car phone holder with up to 15W wireless charging capability. The NFC functionality of the MagSafe car phone holder adds even more convenience. With three NFC shortcuts at your disposal, you can rapidly navigate to your pre-selected apps by simply flicking the relevant shortcut. The S24 car phone holder elevates the interior of your car with a touch of sophistication thanks to its sleek profile and simple aramid fiber patterns.

Samsung Galaxy S24 Charger: Super-Fast and Efficient

Despite the powerful features of your Galaxy S24, continuous use depends on keeping it charged throughout the day. The Galaxy S24 can charge at a lightning-fast 25W rate. That being said, the S24 will charge more quickly and efficiently thanks to the excellent 30W USB-C GaN Charger from PITAKA. In addition, the Galaxy S24 charger can be used with a variety of fast charging protocols, such as PD (Power Delivery), and it can be used with Apple, Android, and Nintendo Switch devices. Additionally, the S24 fast charger's recycled aramid fiber shell ensures outstanding durability and enhances the device's aesthetic appeal. Because of its lightweight and compact design, the charger can easily fit into any pocket or bag, thanks to Gallium Nitride (GaN) technology.

Charging the battery

When using a battery for the first time or after prolonged periods of inactivity, ensure you get it properly charged.

Wired charging

To charge the battery in the device, plug the USB cable into the multipurpose jack and connect it to the USB power adapter. Once the device has finished charging, remove the charger.

Wireless charging

A wireless charging coil is integrated into the device. A wireless charger (separately sold) can be used to charge the battery. To charge the battery, place the device's back center onto the wireless charger's center. Disconnect the device from the wireless charger once it has finished charging. The notification panel will display the estimated charging time. The actual charging time may differ based on the charging conditions and is based on the assumption that the device is not in use. Depending on the kind of cover or accessory, wireless charging might not function properly. It is advised to take the cover or accessory off of the device to achieve stable wireless charging. Below are basic precautions for wireless charging that you should ensure you adhere strictly to. If you don't take the necessary precautions, the device might not charge correctly, it might overheat, or it might break any cards.

- A credit card or radio-frequency identification (RFID) card (such as a transit card or a key card) should never be inserted between the back of the device and the device cover when using a wireless charger.
- When conductive materials, like metal objects or magnets, are positioned between the device and the wireless charger, do not place the device on the charger.
- You run the risk of losing network reception if you use the wireless charger in places with spotty network signals.
- Use wireless chargers approved by Samsung. It is possible that the battery won't charge fully if you use different wireless chargers.

Quick charging

Make use of a fast or ultra-fast charger. Use a charger and compatible parts to take advantage of the fast wireless charging feature.

- To verify the charger's connection state, navigate to **Settings and select Battery.**

- If you are unable to achieve fast charging, go to **Settings,** select **Battery > Charging settings** and then make sure the desired feature is enabled. Additionally, make sure the USB power adapter and USB cable are connected correctly.
- If the gadget or its screen is off, you can charge the battery faster.
- Fast wireless charging may cause the internal fan of the wireless charger to make noise. Create a routine using **Routines** to program the fast wireless charging feature to shut off at a predetermined time. The charger will have less fan noise and an indicator light when the fast wireless charging feature is turned off.

Wireless power-sharing

The battery on your phone can be used to charge another gadget. While your phone is charging, you can continue to charge another device. The wireless power-sharing feature might not function properly depending on the kind of covers or accessories being used. It is advised that before utilizing this feature, all covers and accessories be taken off.

- To enable wireless power sharing, open the notification panel, swipe down, and then tap **Wireless power sharing**.

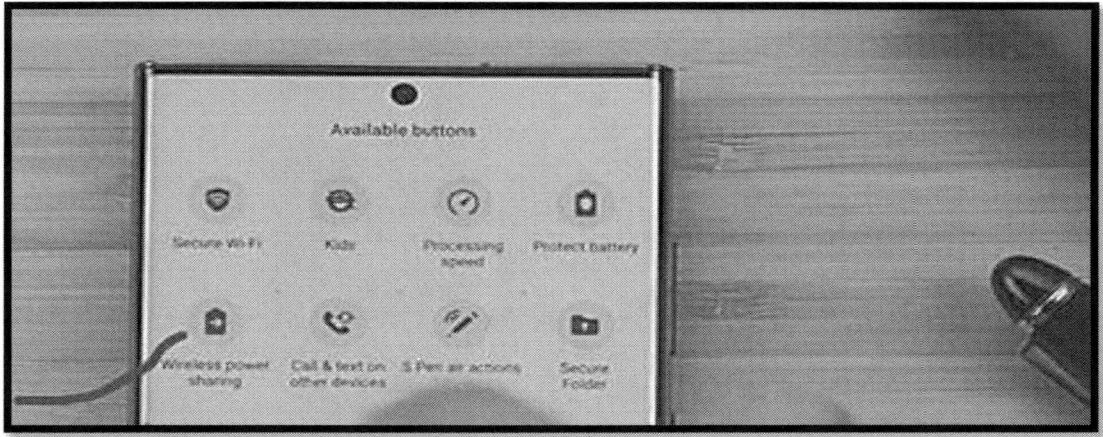

- If the quick settings panel does not have (Wireless power sharing), select > **Edit and drag the button to add it.**
- With their backs to you, position the other device in the center of your phone.
- Ensure you get the other gadget disconnected from your phone when you are done charging.

Whenever you are making use of the wireless sharing power option, ensure you do not make use of headphones as this can affect other devices that are close by.

Take note of the following precautions also;

- Depending on the device, the wireless charging coil's location may vary.
- To ensure that the charging coils connect correctly, adjust the devices.
- While power is shared, certain features are not accessible.
- This feature can only be used to charge devices that support wireless charging. A few gadgets might not have a charge. Visit the Samsung website to view the devices that support the Wireless power-sharing feature.
- Don't move or use either device while it's charging to ensure proper charging.
- The other device's power charge may be lower than the amount your phone shares with it.
- Depending on the type of charger, charging another device while charging your phone may result in a decrease in charging speed or an improper charge for the device.

The gadget can be configured to cease power sharing when the battery life falls below a predetermined threshold. To set the limit, open **Settings, touch Battery**

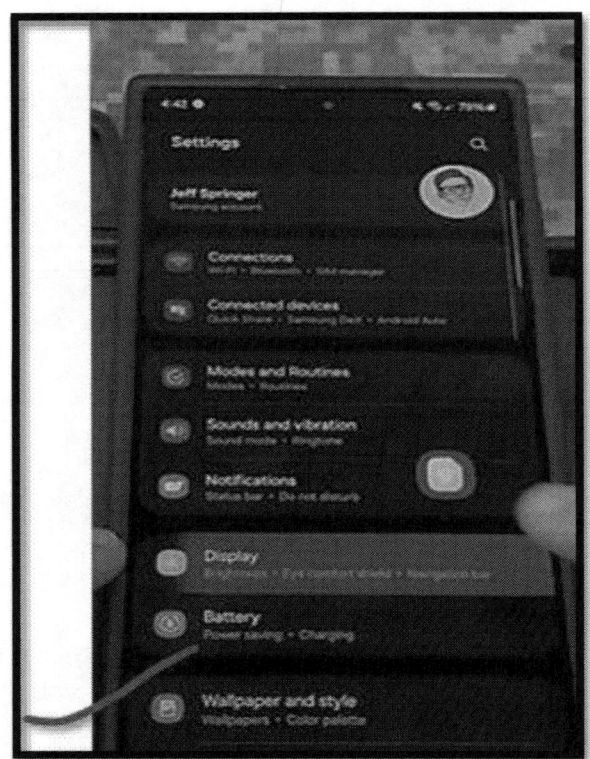

, select Wireless power-sharing > Battery limits, and then enters the desired amount.

Reducing battery consumption

Several options on your device can help you save battery life.

- Utilize the device care feature to maximize the device.
- Press the **Side button** to turn off the screen when you're not using the device.

- Activate the energy-saving mode.
- Shut down any unused apps.
- When not in use, turn off the Bluetooth feature.
- Disable the necessary apps' automatic syncing.
- Cut the duration of the backlight.
- Reduce the brightness of the screen.

Battery charging tips and precautions

Make sure the battery, charger, and cable you use are all made specifically for your device and approved by Samsung. Incompatible batteries, chargers, and cables have the potential to seriously harm you or your device.

- If the charger is not connected correctly, the device could sustain significant harm. The warranty does not cover damage brought on by abuse.

- Only use the USB Type-C cable that came with the gadget. If you use a Micro USB cable, the device might get damaged.
- The gadget might be harmed if it is charged with the multipurpose jack wet. Before charging the device, make sure the multipurpose jack is completely dry.
- When the charger is not in use, unplug it to conserve energy. Since there is no power switch on the charger, you must unplug it from the electrical outlet when not in use to prevent power wastage. While charging, the charger should stay handy and close to the electrical outlet.
- When the charger is connected, the device cannot be turned on right away if the battery is fully dead. Before using a discharged battery, give it a few minutes to charge.
- The battery will run out quickly if you use network apps, apps that require a connection to another device, or multiple apps open at once. Use these applications only after the battery has fully charged to prevent power outages during data transfers.
- Given that there is less electric current when using a power source other than the charger, like a computer, the charging speed may be slower.
- The screen might not work if the device is charging with an unstable power source. Unplug the charger from the device if this occurs.
- The gadget and the charger may get heated up during the charging process. This is typical and shouldn't have an impact on the functionality or lifespan of the device. The charger might stop charging if the battery becomes hotter than normal.
- Take the gadget and the charger to a Samsung service center or an authorized service center if the charging process isn't working properly.
- While charging, the device can be used; however, the battery may take longer to charge fully.

Nano-SIM card and eSIM

Put in the USIM or SIM card, or use the eSIM that your carrier has provided. An embedded digital SIM is called an eSIM, and it is different from a physical nano-SIM card. Put in another SIM card, or USIM card, or download another eSIM if you want to use two phone numbers or carriers on the same device.

- eSIM might not be accessible based on the model, carrier, or region.
- Depending on the carrier, some services that need a network connection might not be offered.
- In certain places, using two eSIMs or the nano-SIM card together may result in slower data transfer speeds.

Inserting the SIM or USIM card

- To start with, you need to release the tray by inserting the ejection pin into the hole on the tray.

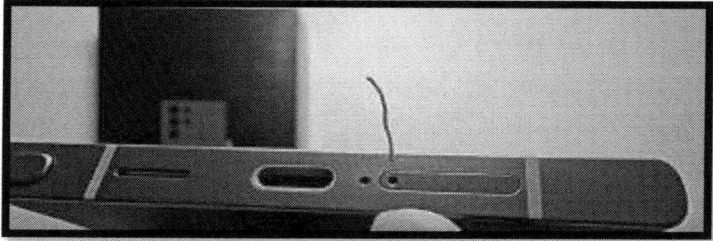

- Gently remove the tray from its designated slot.
- With the gold-colored contacts facing up, place the SIM or USIM card on the tray.

- Press the SIM or USIM card into the tray to ensure it is securely in place.
- Reposition the tray inside its designated slot.
  - To remove the tray, insert the ejection pin into the hole.
  - Only utilize nano-SIM cards.
  - Take care not to misplace or allow someone else to use the USIM or SIM card. Any losses or annoyances brought on by misplaced or stolen cards are not Samsung's fault.
  - Make sure the hole and the ejection pin are perpendicular. If not, there could be damage to the gadget.
  - The SIM card may come loose from the tray or fall out if it is not firmly inserted.
  - Your device might get damaged if you put the tray inside it while it's still wet. Make sure the tray is always dry.
  - Make sure the tray is inserted into the tray slot to keep liquids out of your gadget.

SIM manager (dual SIM models)

Select **Connections > SIM manager after opening Settings**.

- **SIM cards**: Set up your SIM card's settings and activate it for use.
- **eSIMs**: Activate or download the eSIM.
- **Preferred SIMs**: When two SIM cards are activated, you can choose which one to use for particular features like voice calls.
- **Data switching**: If the preferred SIM card is unable to establish a network connection, configure the device to use a different SIM card for data services. When utilizing this feature, you might be charged extra.
- **Additional SIM settings**: Tailor the eSIM or call preferences.

Downloading an eSIM

- Select **Connections**

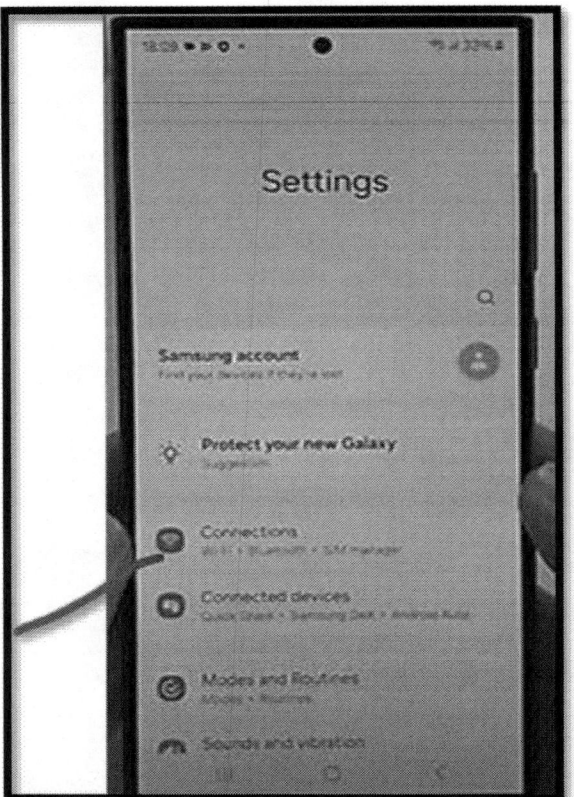

> SIM manager

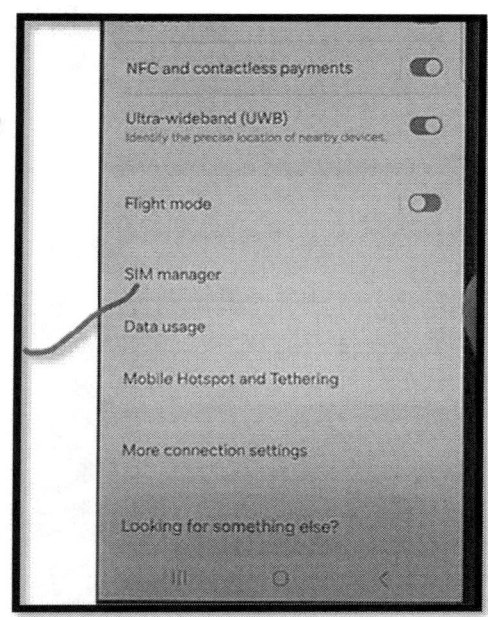

> Add eSIM

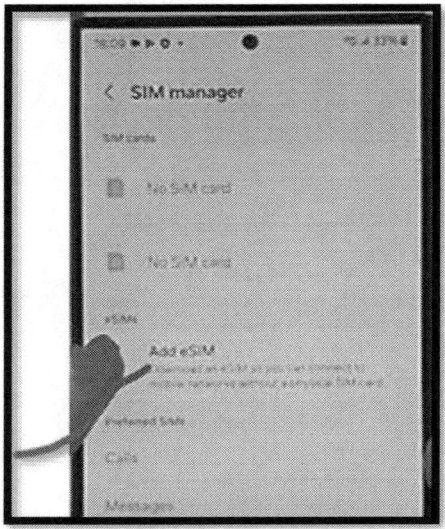

- **After opening Settings**. Once a mobile plan has been identified, download the eSIM by following the on-screen directions.
- Open **Settings, select Connections > SIM manager > Add eSIM > Scan QR code,** and then scan the code if your carrier has given you one.

Turning the device on and off

It is advised that in places where using wireless devices is prohibited, like hospitals and airplanes, heed all posted cautions and instructions from authorized staff.

Switching the device on

- To turn on the device, press and hold the **Side button for a short while.**

Turning the device off

- Press and hold **the Side and Volume Down buttons** at the same time to turn off the device. As an alternative, swipe down to reveal the notification panel, then tap.

- Press the **Power off button.**

- Tap **Restart t**o restart the device.
- Press the **Side button settings**, then select the **Power off menu under Press and hold** if you want to configure the device to turn off whenever you press and hold the **Side button.**

Forcing restart

- To restart your device if it's frozen and unresponsive, press and hold the **Side and Volume Down buttons** at the same time for longer than seven seconds.

Emergency calls and medical information

You have the option to check the medical data you saved or place an emergency call. Hold down both the **Side and Volume Down buttons at the same time, and then select Emergency call or Medical info**.

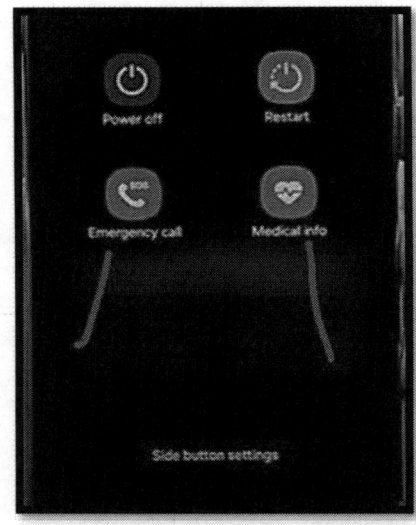

Alternatively, swipe downward to reveal the notification panel, then tap the **Shutdown icon > Emergency call or Medical info.**

- Open S**ettings, select Safety and Emergency,** and manage your medical records and emergency contacts.

Initial setup

Follow the on-screen instructions to set up your device when you turn it on for the first time or after doing a data reset. During the initial setup, you may not be able to configure certain device features if you are not connected to a Wi-Fi network.

Samsung Account

You can use the Samsung account to access a range of Samsung services offered on the Samsung website, TVs, and mobile devices. Go to account.samsung.com to view the list of services that are compatible with your Samsung account.

- **Select Samsung account after opening Settings.** Or, go to **Settings, select Accounts and Backup,**

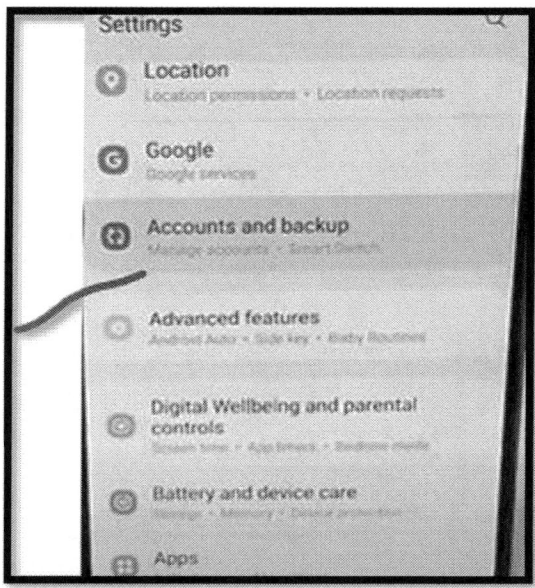

Then Manage accounts,

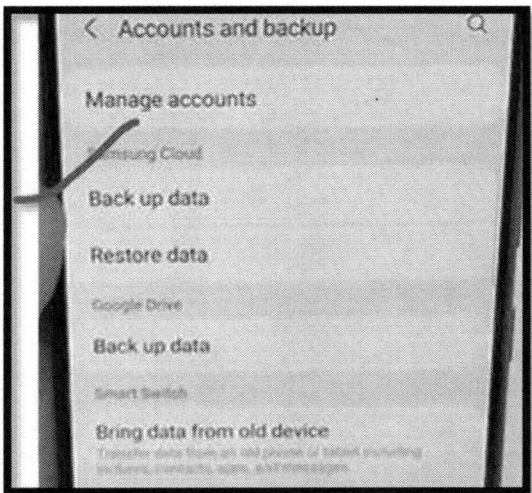

Add account

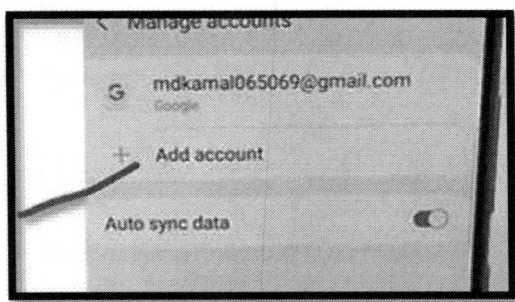

, and finally, Samsung account.

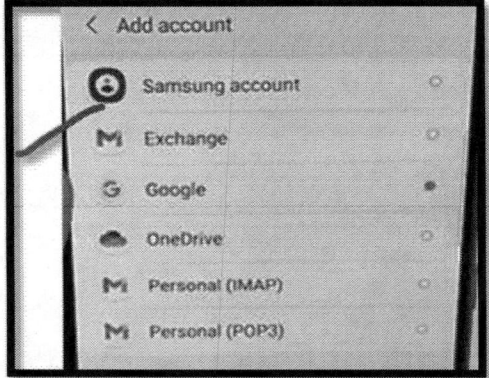

- Open your Samsung account and log in. Select Forgot password or don't have an account? if you don't have a Samsung account then choose **Create an account.**

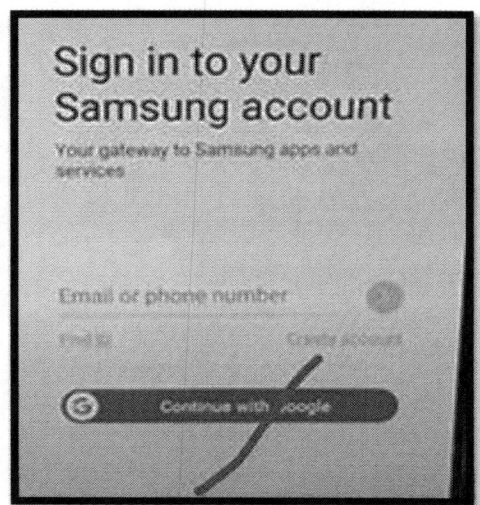

Finding your ID and resetting your password

- Select **Forgot password or don't have an account** if you can't remember your Samsung account ID or password. The sign-in screen for your Samsung account may say Forgot ID or Forgot password.

After you've entered the necessary data, you can retrieve your ID or change your password.

Singing out of your Samsung account

Your contacts and events will be deleted from your device along with your data when you log out of your Samsung account.

- Select **Accounts and Backup > Manage accounts after opening Settings**.
- Select **My profile under Samsung account**, then click **Sign out** at the lower part of the screen.
- Select **Sign out,** type in the password for your Samsung account, and select **OK**.

Transferring data from your previous device

Transferring data from your old phone to your new one is possible with Smart Switch.

- To set up your device, navigate to **Settings**, then tap **Accounts and Backup > Transfer data.**
- To view the transferred data, select **more (three dots) > Transfer result.**
  - Certain computers or devices might not support this feature.
  - Restrictions are in place. To learn more, go to www.samsung.com/smartswitch. Copyright is a serious matter for Samsung. Transferring content should only be done with permission or ownership.

Transferring data using a USB cable

To transfer data, use the USB cable to connect your old phone to your new one. Download the app from the Play Store or Galaxy Store if it wasn't on your old device.

- Make sure the USB cable on your new phone is connected to the old device. Depending on the prior device, a USB connector might be required.
- After the pop-up window displaying the app selection appears, select **Smart Switch**

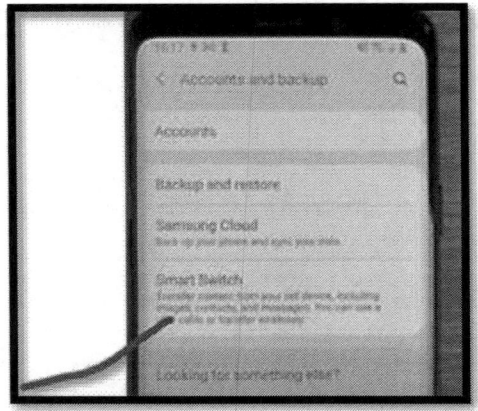

> Receive data.

- Press **Allow** on the previous device. When your new phone detects the old one, a list of data that you can transfer will show up.
- To transfer data from your new phone, choose an option, hit **Next,** and then adhere to the on-screen directions.

Note: When transferring files, keep the USB cable connected to the device. Data loss or device damage could result from not doing this. Your device's battery usage increases when you transfer data. Make sure your device has enough battery life before sending any data. Data transfer may stop if the battery is low on power.

Transferring data wirelessly

Wi-Fi Direct allows you to wirelessly transfer data from your old phone to your new one.

- Open the **Smart Switch app** on the previous device. Get the app from the Play Store or Galaxy Store if you don't already have it.
- To set up your device, go to Settings on your new phone, select **Accounts and Backup, and then select Transfer data.**
- Position the gadgets close to one another.
- On the earlier gadget, select **Send data > Wireless.**

- Choose the operating system of your previous device by tapping **Receive data** on your new phone, and then tap **Wireless.**
- Press **Connect** on the previous device.
- To transfer data from your new phone, choose an option, hit **Next,** and then adhere to the on-screen directions.

Accounts and backup

On the Settings screen, tap **Accounts and Backup**. You can also sign in to accounts, like your Samsung account or Google account, and use Smart Switch to transfer data to and from other devices. You can use Samsung Cloud to sync, back up, or restore data on your device.

- **Manage accounts:** Add additional accounts to sync with, such as your Google and Samsung accounts.
- **Samsung Cloud**: Create a backup of your data and settings, and even if you lose it, restore the data and settings from the prior device.

- **Google Drive**: Safeguard your device's settings, app data, and personal information. You can back up your private data. To backup data, you need to sign into your Google account.

Make regular backups of your data to a computer or secure location, like Samsung Cloud, so you can recover it if an unintentional factory data reset causes data loss or damage.

Backing up data

The data on your device can be backed up to Samsung Cloud.

- Select **Accounts, backup, and then select Back up data under Samsung Cloud from the Settings screen.**
- To back up items, tap the switches next to them, then select **Back up now.**
- **Click "Done."**
  - Not all of the data will be backed up. On the Settings screen, select **Accounts and Backup, then select Back up data under Samsung Cloud to see which data will be backed up.**
  - Choose a device from the list by tapping **Accounts and Backup > Restore data** on the Settings screen to view the backup data for other devices in your Samsung Cloud.

Restoring data

You can use Samsung Cloud to restore your device's backup data.

- Select **Accounts and Backup from the Settings screen.**
- Choose your preferred device by tapping **Restore data.**

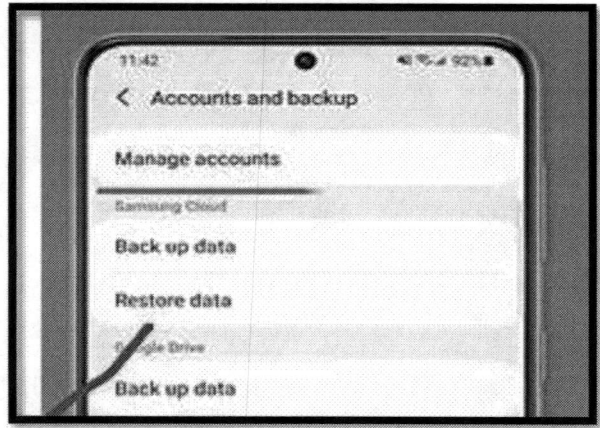

- Select the objects you wish to get back and click **Restore.**

Tips to Consider to Consider When Making Use of the Phone

- Avoid putting the device near your ears when you're using the speakers, such as when playing media files or utilizing a speakerphone.
- Take care not to expose the camera lens to bright light sources like the sun. The image sensor of the camera could be harmed if it is subjected to intense light, like sunlight. An irreparable image sensor damage will result in dots or spots in images.
- Use of the device with a broken glass or acrylic body could result in harm. Only use the device once it has been fixed at an authorized service center or a Samsung service center.
- The sound on the device may become muffled or certain features may stop working if dust or foreign objects get inside the microphone, speaker, or receiver, or if these components are covered. Using a sharp object to try and remove the dust or foreign materials could cause damage to the device and change its appearance.
- **Issues with connectivity and low battery life may arise in the following scenarios:**
  - When you affix metallic stickers to the device's antenna section
  - When a metallic device cover is attached to a device.
  - When making calls or using a mobile data connection, for example, if you cover the antenna area of the device with your hands or something else.
- Unwanted noises may sound during calls or media playback if the air vent hole is covered by an accessory, like a protective film or sticker.
- Avoid covering the proximity/light sensor area with covers or other accessories. By doing this, the sensor might stop working.
- During calls, the device's top light may flicker due to proximity sensor operation.

Activity

1. Mention 3 features of the Samsung Galaxy S24 Ultra, S24 Plus, and S24.
2. List 5 accessories you can use with the Samsung S24.
3. Charge the battery of your phone before you turn it on.
4. Insert your SIM card into your phone.
5. Turn your device on so start making use of it.
6. Create a Samsung Account.
7. Transfer data from your previous phone to your new phone.
8. Back up your phone to ensure that the information saved on it is not lost.

CHAPTER 2

NAVIGATION AROUND THE SAMSUNG S24 SERIES

The Home Screen and App screen

All of the features on the device can be accessed from the Home screen. It shows widgets, app shortcuts, and other information. All apps, including recently installed ones, have icons displayed on the Apps screen.

Switching between Home and Apps screens

Swipe up to reveal the Applications screen from the Home screen. Swipe up or down on the Applications screen to get back to the Home screen. As an alternative, you can also choose to tap the **Back or Home buttons.**

- Tapping the **Apps button** on the Home screen will allow you to access the A**pps screen**. To enable the Show Apps screen button on the Home screen switch, touch and hold an empty area on the screen, select **Settings**, and then tap the **button**. At the bottom of the Home screen, an Apps button will be added.

Editing the Home screen

To access the editing options on the Home screen, pinch your fingers together or touch and hold an empty area. In addition, you can add widgets and change the wallpaper. Also, you can reorganize, add, or remove Home screen panels.

- **Adding panels: To add a panel, swipe left and then press.**
- **Panel movement**: Drag **the preview of a panel to a new location.**
- **Panel deletion**: Press **the panel.**

Style and wallpaper: Here you can modify the locked screen and the home screen's wallpaper.

Theme: In this option, you get to modify the theme on the gadget. Depending on the theme chosen, the interface's visual components—such as colors, icons, and wallpaper—will alter.

Widgets: On your Home screen, widgets are little applications that initiate particular app functionalities to offer information and easy access. After choosing a widget, click **Add**. The Home screen will now have the widget.

Settings: In the settings option you get to adjust the Home screen's configuration, including the screen arrangement.

Display all apps on the Home screen

You can configure the device to show all apps on the Home screen in place of a separate Apps screen.

- Touch and hold any space on the **Home screen, then select Settings > Home screen layout > Home screen only > Apply.**

Finder

With the use of the finder, you can locate content on the device.

- Tap **Search on the Apps screen.**
- Put a keyword in here. Your device's content and apps will be looked through. You can look for more content by tapping the keyboard's search icon.

Moving items

In this section, you can drag an object to a different place. You can also drag the item to the side of the screen to transfer it to a different panel. You can select multiple items at once and move them together by touching and holding an item and then tapping Select. Touch and hold an **app on the Apps screen**, then select **Add to Home** to add a shortcut to the app on the Home screen. The app will have a shortcut added to the Home screen. Additionally, you can relocate often-used apps to the Home screen's shortcuts section.

Creating folders

You can drag one app over another on the Apps or Home screens.

- The chosen apps will be placed in a brand-new folder. To enter a folder name, tap the **Folder name.**
- **Add more apps**: touch the add icon on the folder. Choose the apps you would like to add by ticking the boxes and then once completed, touch Done. You can also choose to include an app by moving it to the folder.
- **Moving apps from a folder:** you can move an app to a new location.
- **Deleting a folder**: Select **Delete Folder** after touching and holding a folder. The folder alone will be erased. The apps in the folder will move to the Apps screen.

Edge panel

From the Edge panels, you can access your favorite features and apps. Move the Edge panel handle in the direction of the screen's center.

- To enable the Edge panel handle if it's not visible, navigate to **Settings, select Display,**

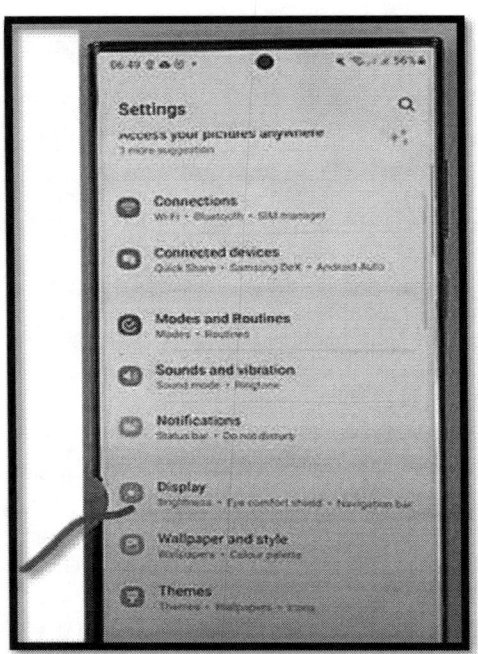

And then press the Edge panel switch.

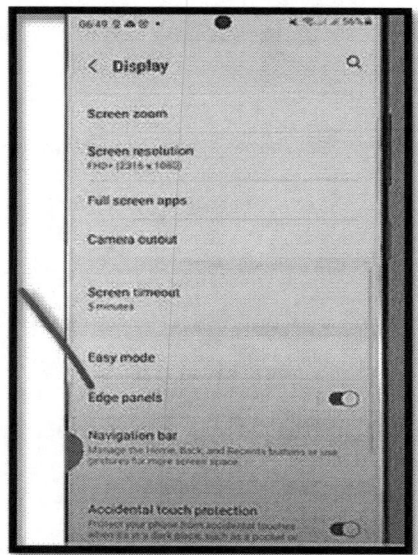

Controlling the TouchScreen

There are various ways through which you can get to control the screen of your Samsung Galaxy S24.

Some of these methods will be highlighted and briefly explained in the sections below;

- **Tapping:** here all you get to do is simply touch the screen. It is often used to launch an application.
- **Dragging**: you make use of this option to move an item to the target position.
- **Swiping**: Slide in any direction—up, down, left, or right.
- **Touching** and holding: Press and **hold the screen for about two seconds.**
- **Double tapping**: tap **the screen twice.**
- **Spreading and pinching:** Pinch or **spread apart two fingers on the screen.**

Please take note of the following when making use of the screen;

- Avoid letting the screen make contact with any other electrical equipment. Electrostatic discharges may result in malfunctioning of the screen.
- Avoid tapping the screen with anything sharp or applying too much pressure to your fingertips or another object to prevent damage.
- It is advised that you should not make use of fixed graphics on any portion of the screen for prolonged periods. Ghosting or afterimages (screen burn-in) could occur from doing this.

Notification panel

The status bar displays indicator icons when you receive new notifications. To see them just open the notification panel and look over the details to see additional information about the icons.

- Drag **the status bar down to reveal the notification panel.** To dismiss the notification panel, swipe the screen upward.

Utilizing the Quick Settings Panel

To access the quick settings panel, swipe downward on the notification panel. To toggle a particular feature on or off, tap **the button**. To view more specific settings, either touch and hold a button or tap its text.

- Tap the **pen icon > Edit to edit buttons.**

Controlling media playback

You can utilize the notification panel to manage media on your phone and other nearby connected devices.

- Press **Media output** when the notification panel opens.

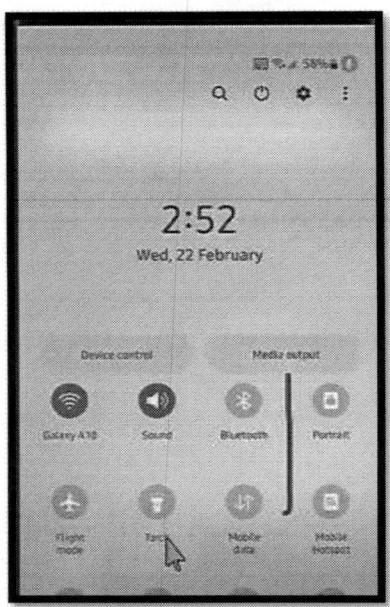

- To control the playback, tap the **controller's icons.**

Controlling nearby devices

From the notification panel, start and manage frequently used SmartThings devices, manual routines, and nearby connected devices.

- Select **Device Control** after bringing up the notification panel. There will be an appearance of nearby connected devices, SmartThings devices, and manual routines.

- To control it, choose a nearby device, a SmartThings device, or start it manually by selecting **a manual routine**.

Screen capture and screen record

Screen capture

While using the device, take a screenshot and use the captured screen to annotate, illustrate, crop, or share. Both the scrollable area and the active screen can be captured.

Capturing a screenshot

To take a screenshot, use the techniques listed below. The screenshots that were taken can be viewed in the Gallery.

- **Button capture**: Press the **Volume Down and Side buttons** at the same time.
- **Swipe capture**: Move your hand to the left or right across the screen using the edge of your hand. If you want to enable the ability to take screenshots by swiping, go to **Settings**, select **Advanced features**

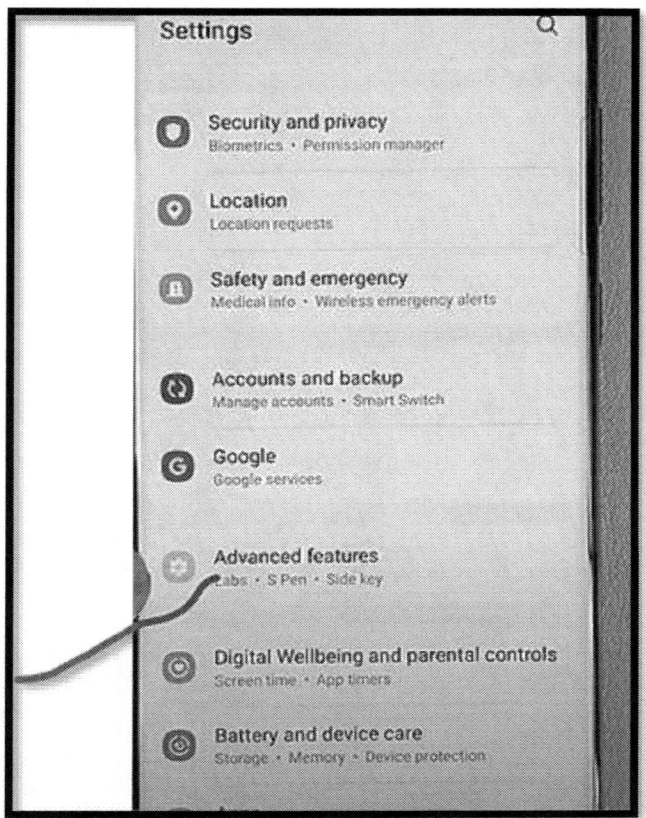

> Motions and gestures,

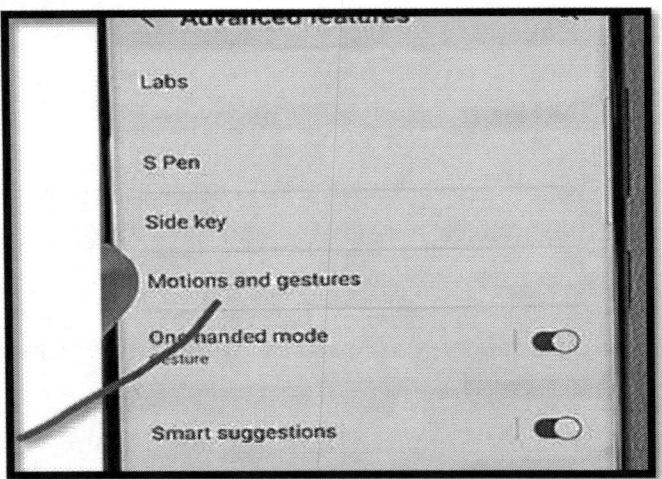

And then turn on the **Palm swipe** to capture features by tapping **the switch.**

After you have captured a screenshot, you are free to do any of the following with the use of the toolbar at the bottom of the screen;

- Take pictures of the visible content and the content that is hidden on an extended page, like a webpage. The screen will automatically scroll down when you tap, capturing more content.
- You can write or draw on the screenshot, or you can crop a section of it. The cropped area is visible in the Gallery.
- Give the screenshot some tags. To find screenshots by tag, repeatedly tap the Gallery's search field. You can look through the tags list and find the desired screenshot.

Screen record

Take screen captures while using your device.

- Swipe down to reveal the notification panel, then tap the **Screen recorder.**

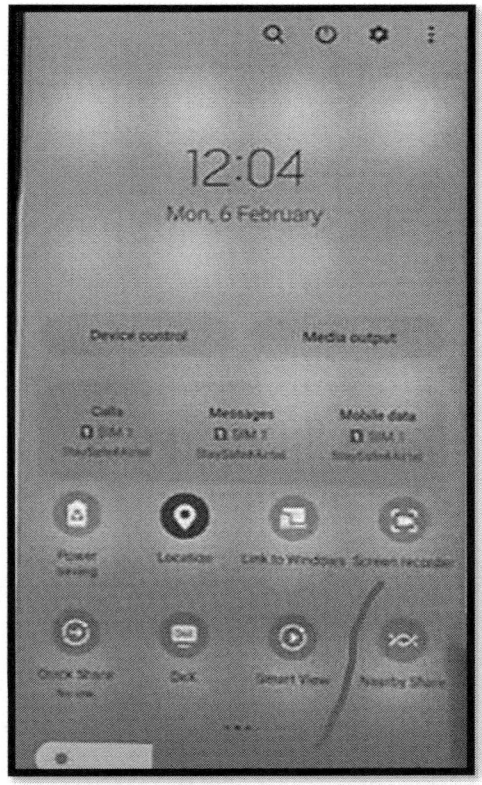

- After choosing a sound option, click "**Start recording.**" A countdown will ensue before the recording begins.

- You can **tap the screen to write or draw.**
- o Press the arrow icon to display the S Pen pointer on the screen. This function is only available when the S Pen is not attached to the device. (Model: Galaxy S24 Ultra)
- Tap **to record the screen with your video overlay.**
- o Once the video has finished recording, press **the stop recording icon**. Check out the video in the Gallery.

Entering text

Keyboard layout

When you enter text, a keyboard appears automatically. Some languages do not support text entry; you must switch the input language to one of the supported languages to enter text.

Change the input language

o Choose the languages to be used by tapping **Settings > Languages and types**

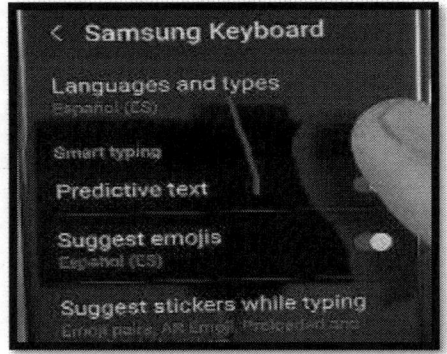

Manage input languages.

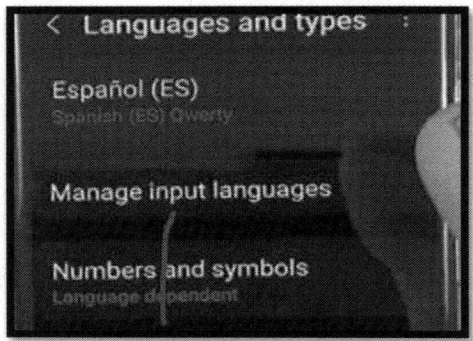

You can use tapping to switch between the input languages when you have more than one language selected. To modify the keyboard type, go to **Settings > Languages and Types**, choose your preferred language, and then pick the desired keyboard type.

Using the keyboard button

To modify the text input method, simply tap the keyboard button located on the navigation bar. To modify the keyboard button on the navigation bar, press and hold **it while choosing your preferred option.**

- If the keyboard button is absent from the navigation bar, navigate to **Settings, select General Management > Keyboard list and default, and then select the keyboard button to activate it from the navigation bar switch.**

Copying and pasting

- Hold and touch the text.
- To pick the text you want, drag it or tap **Select All to pick it all.**
- Select **Copy or Cut by tapping**. Copying the chosen text to the clipboard occurs.
- To insert the text, touch and hold the desired location, then select **Paste**. To insert previously copied text, tap **Clipboard and choose the text.**

Extracting text

Certain apps, like the Gallery or Camera app, allow you to extract text from images and apply functions like copying and sharing. The actions listed below demonstrate how to extract text in the Gallery application.

- Press when viewing an image in the Gallery app. Only when there is text to extract does the icon appear.
- To extract text, select an area.
- Choose the option that appeals to you.

Activity

1. Navigate around the home and app screen of your device.
2. Control the touchscreen of your device; tap, drag, swipe, touch, and hold, and also double tap on your touchscreen.
3. Make use of the quick settings panel to edit buttons.
4. Control the media playback and the devices close to you.
5. Make use of the button and swipe capture on your device.
6. Type a text on your phone with the use of the keyboard.
7. Extract text from a certain area of your phone.

CHAPTER 3

TRANSFER CONTENT WITH SAMSUNG SMART SWITCH

Loss of important items such as pictures, music, videos, notes, documents, etc. is one of the major reasons why most people will prefer to stick to their device no matter how outdated it is. Important documents often get missing during a swap depending on the importance of the file it can be very sad having to lose such files. With the amazing Samsung switch, you don't have to worry about your old documents as you can have them transferred with ease to your new device. Say no to the loss of files today with the Samsung switch and get ready to transfer your files to your new phone without missing any.

- Open **Settings > Touch Accounts and Backup > Bring data from the old device**.

Wireless transfer from Android phone

You can transfer your files wireless with the use of Wi-Fi Direct. With this, you are sure **your device will receive all of the data and there will be no fear of a cord getting detached which can lead to loss of data.**

- Open **SmartSwitch** on the former phone. Download from either the Galaxy store or the Play store if you do not have it.
- Go to your new phone and open **Settings > Touch Accounts and Backup> Bring data from the old device**.
- Ensure the devices are positioned beside each other. This is to enhance the speed of the transfer.
- On the former device, touch **Send data > Wireless**.

- On your new phone, touch Receive data, choose your former device operating system then touch the **Wireless option**.
- Go to the former device and touch **Allow**.
- On your new phone choose your preferred option and touch Next then follow the instructions shown on the screen to complete the data transfer.

Import content from iCloud

You've concluded that your time spent using Apple products is done. If you want to give Android a try, a Samsung phone looks like the most secure bet. After all, they are the largest manufacturer and have a line of watches, making it easy to find a suitable alternative to the Apple Watch. The question is, how can you get data from an iPhone to a Samsung? Although a clean slate is always an option, chances are you'll want to bring some familiar documents over to your new best buddy. Here's how to make the switch without a USB cord as painless as possible. Even if you don't have a USB cable or your Samsung's battery is below 60%, you can still utilize Smart Switch over Wi-Fi. You can find this option in your Samsung setup wizard, or you may download the Samsung Smart Switch app. For this to function, both gadgets must be linked to the same wireless network. **The procedure is as follows:**

- Open **Smart Switch** on your **Samsung device** and touch **Get data from iCloud instead**.

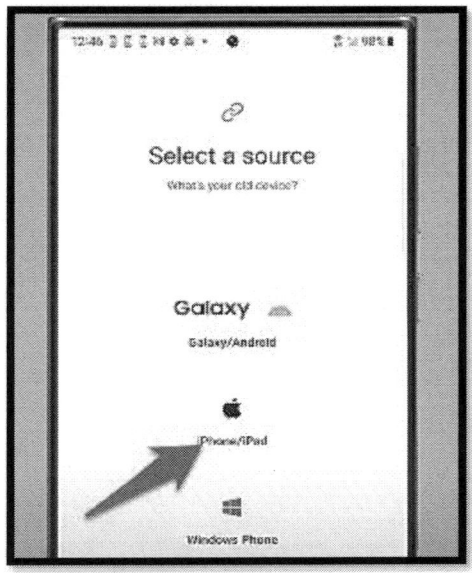

- Sign in to your **iCloud account** then insert the verification code to gain access to your data.

- The data in your iPhone will commence transfer instantly.

Once the transfer has been completed, your data will be displayed on your Samsung phone and it will also still be intact on your iPhone. Note that music and videos purchased from iTunes cannot be moved to iCloud. If you have an unprotected iTunes library on a computer, you can easily transfer the music to your phone by copying the M4A files to your phone's storage. Your music collection can also be transferred from a personal computer.

Connect your devices using a USB Cable

It is recommended that your devices have at least a 20% charge before using Smart Switch over a USB OTG connection. It could be a while before the transfer is complete if there is a lot of multimedia data to move. The transfer will go more smoothly if your devices are fully charged. Individuals who don't have a lot of information stored on their old phones should use the wired transfer method. This is because, during a wired transfer, you cannot have your phones plugged into a charger. It is advised you follow the wireless transfer route if you have a lot of data or many years' worth of text messages to move.

- Connect the phones with the **USB cable of the old phone**. Most of the cables will require you to make use of a USB-OTG adapter. If you possess an iPhone that has a Lightning to USB-C or an Android with a USB-C to USB-C cable, there will be no need for an adapter; it will be plugged into your Galaxy straight away.
- Open the **Smart Switch on the two phones**. On your new Galaxy phone, open **Settings > Locate Smart Switch then touches Bring data from the old device. Touch Bring data from an old device once more**.

46

Go to the old phone, touch **Send data > touch Cable**.

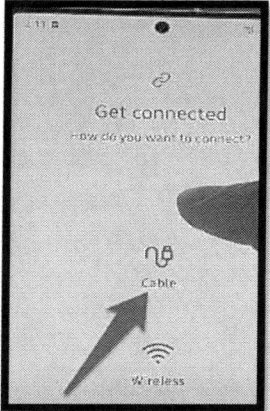

- On the new phone, touch **Receive data, choose the specific type of device you're transferring data from i.e. Galaxy/Android then touch Cable**. Smart Switch will commence scanning the old phone for contents that can be transferred.
- Specify **the data** you wish to move to the new phone after the scan is complete. The estimated duration of the data transfer will be shown. It's recommended to use a wireless transfer if the transfer will require more than an hour, as this will allow both phones to be charged while the transfer is ongoing.
- When you are set to commence, touch **transfer**.

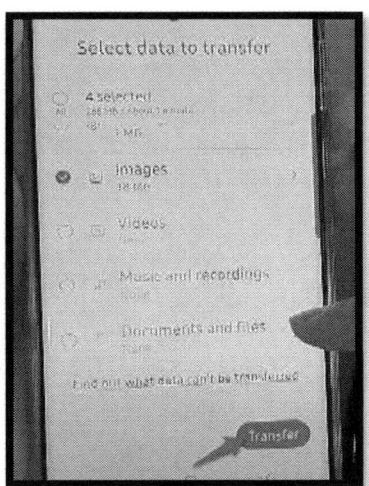

- When the transfer has been completed, touch **Done** on the new phone then touch **Close on the old phone.**

Using a MicroSD card or USB Flash drive

You can connect your device to your new phone with the use of a USB cable to transfer data.

- Connect your new phone and the former one with the use of the USB cable of the new phone. There might be a need for a USB connector based on the type of the former device.
- Upon the display of the app selection, touch **Smart Switch > Receive data**.
- Go to the previous data and touch **OK**. If you do not have the app on your device you can download it from either the Galaxy Store or the Play Store. Your phone will immediately recognize the device and will display a list of data you can transfer.
- **On your new phone, choose your preferred option touch Next then follow the instructions displayed on the screen to transfer data.**
  - Keep the device attached to the device through the USB cord at all times during the transfer process. The risk of losing data or damaging the gadget increases when this is not done.
  - As the amount of data you transfer grows, so does the drain on your battery. When transferring information, make sure your device has enough juice. Insufficient battery power might cause disruptions in data transmission.

For an SD card, follow the instructions below;

- Open **the Smart Switch** on the old phone. On the new Galaxy phone, open **Settings > Locate Smart Switch then touch Bring data from the old device. Touch Bring data from the old device again**.
- Touch the **SD card icon** located in the upper right corner then touch the **SD card beneath Back up.**
- Choose the specific things you would like to have backed up. If the space happens to be insufficient, you might just have to deselect some items but you can transfer anything that won't fit much later.
- You can choose just anything you want; calls, contacts, and messages. Once done touch **Next.** If a pop message is displayed, choose **the right option**.
- Follow the instructions on the screen. Although it might vary based on the option you choose. When that is done, touch **Done** then take off the **SD card**.
- Next, put the **SD card** into the new Galaxy phone and open the **Smart Switch**.
- Touch the **icon of the SD card then touch Restore**. Choose what you would like to restore the tap Restore once more.

- When all of that is complete, choose Next then touch **Done**. You can take this process as many times as you would like to.

To copy data from your device to an external hard drive, you can use a file explorer application, such as My Files, while your device is connected to the hard drive through an OTG cable. For Galaxy devices to read data from an external hard drive, it must be formatted in either FAT or exFAT. An external power source is necessary for some portable hard disk devices.

How to copy Data from Windows Phone

The Smart Switch can also be used to transfer data from a Windows phone.

- Go to the new Galaxy phone, open **Settings > locate Smart Switch then touch Bring data from old device. Tap Bring data from the old device again**.

- On the new Galaxy phone, touch **Receive data then touch Windows Phone**.

- You will then see steps to download the Smart Switch software to your old device. Follow the instructions on your screen to continue. Your location device will need to be turned on if it isn't before.
- Upon the installation of your Smart Switch, open and touch **Connect** on the Old phone then choose the network.
- Insert the password displayed on your new Galaxy phone. Your data transfer will then commence.

Transferring Backup Data from a Computer

You can back up data from your former device to a computer and then import the data to your new phone.

- Get on the computer, visit www.samsung.com/smartswitch to have Smart Switch downloaded on the computer.
- On your computer, open **Smart Switch**. If the device you were using before is not s Samsung device backup data to the computer following instructions from the manufacturer of the device. Once done skip to the fifth step.
- Connect your former device to the computer with the use of the USB cable of the device.
- Back up your device's data to your computer by following the on-screen prompts. Afterward, remove the earlier device from the computer.
- Connect your new phone to the computer with the use of the **USB cable**.
- Follow the on-screen instructions on the computer to transfer data to your new phone.

Activity

1. Make a wireless transfer of some files from an Android phone to your device.
2. Import files from iCloud to your device.
3. Connect your device to a computer with the use of the USB cable.
4. Copy data from a Windows phone to your phone.

CHAPTER 4

PHONE

Make a phone call

- Click the **Keypad when the Phone app is open.**
- Put a phone number in here.
- To place a voice call, tap **the green call icon. To place a video call, tap the video or Google Meet icons.**

Making calls from call logs or contacts list

- To make a call, launch **the Phone app,**

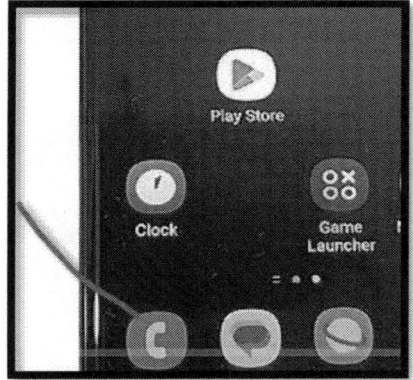

Select **Recent or Contacts,**

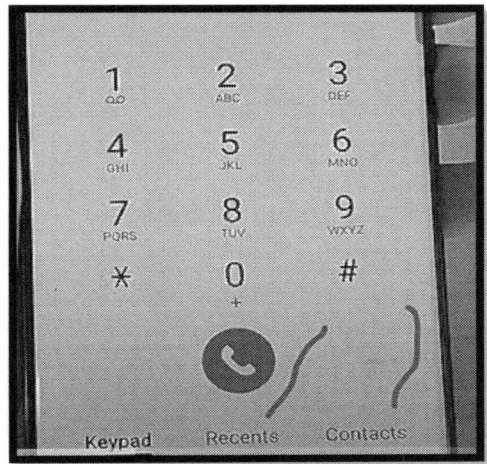

And then swipe right on a contact or phone number.

- If you would like to enable this feature, go to **More Options > Settings > Other call settings, and then select the Swipe to call or text option.**

Using speed dial

- Open the Phone app, select **Keypad > More options > Speed dial numbers, choose a speed dial number, and then add a phone number to set a number to speed dial.**

Press and hold a speed dial number on the keypad to place a call. For speed dial numbers 10 and higher, touch and hold the final digit after tapping the first digit or digits. For instance, if you have speed dialed 123, tap 1, tap 2, and then touch and hold 3.

Making an international call

- Click the **Keypad when the Phone app is open**.
- Press and **hold 0 to make the plus sign appear.**

- After entering the phone number, area code, and nation code, presses the green call icon.

Answering phone calls

To answer a phone call, all you need to do is drag the call icon outside the large circle.

Reject a call

- To reject a call, **drag the red call icon outside the big circle** whenever a call comes in. When you reject an incoming call, you can drag the Send message bar up and choose which message to send.

Open the **Phone app, select More options > Settings > Quick decline messages**, type a message, and then tap to create a variety of rejection messages.

How to Block a number

Put specific numbers on your block list and prevent calls from them.

- To save contacts or phone numbers in the blocked numbers list, launch the **Phone app, tap > More options > Settings > Block numbers**, and then choose which **contacts or numbers to save**.

You won't be notified when blocked numbers attempt to reach you. The conversations will appear in the call log. Incoming calls from individuals who do not display their caller ID can also be blocked. To activate the feature, tap the Block calls from unknown numbers then switch on the feature.

Options during calls

- **Call assistance > Text call:** Text the other person to establish communication.
- **Call assistance > live translate**: During voice calls, get translations into the language of your choice in real time. Open the Phone app, select the **phone app icon > More Options > Settings > Live translate**, and then tap the switch to activate this feature.
- **Add call**: Place a follow-up call. We're going to put the first call on hold. The first call will resume when the second call ends.
- **Hold call**: Place a call on hold.
- **Video call**: Make a video call now.
- **Bluetooth:** If your headset is linked to the device, switch to it.
- **Speaker:** Turn on or off the speakerphone. Avoid putting the speakerphone close to your ears when using it.
- **Mute:** To prevent the other person from hearing you, turn off the microphone.
- **Keypad / Hide**: Slide the keypad open or closed.
- **Effects**: Use a variety of effects when on a video call.
- **Camera**: To ensure that the other person cannot see you during a video call, turn off the camera.
- **Switch**: Alternate between the front and rear cameras when on a video call.

Call Assist

Text call

- Text the other party to establish communication. To make or receive a text call while on the phone, select **Call Assist > Text Call.**

The other party automatically receives a voice greeting when the call is connected, and your screen displays text from the other party. The other party will hear your response if you type text or choose an answer from the quick response list. Swipe right on the call screen and select Switch to voice call to transition to a voice call.

- Open the Phone app, then select **More Options > Settings > Text call to modify the settings.**

Live translate

During voice calls, get real-time translation into the language of your choice. Open the **Phone app, select More options**

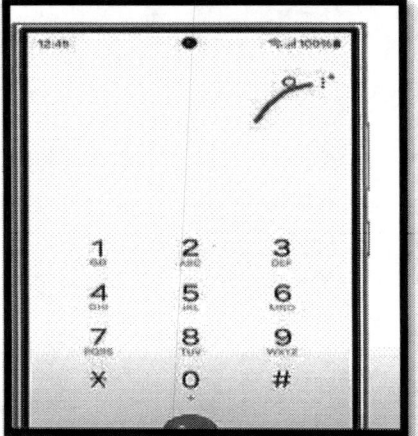

> **Settings**

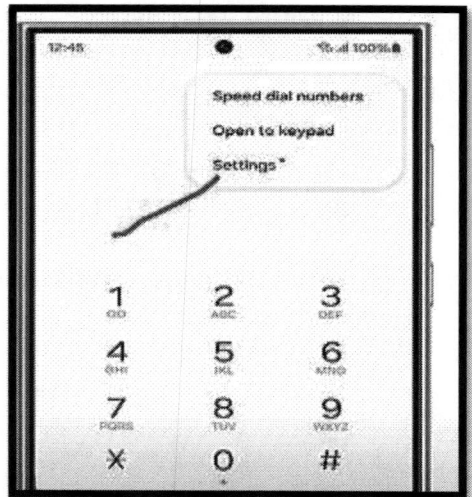

> Live translate,

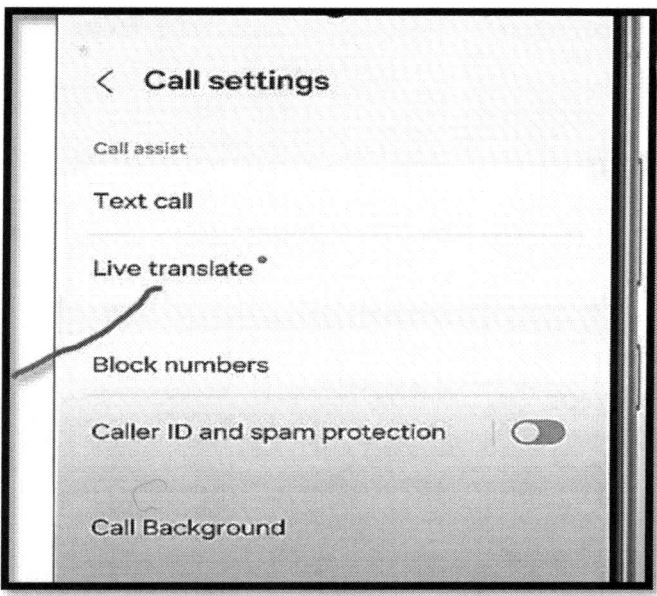

And then select the switch to enable this feature.

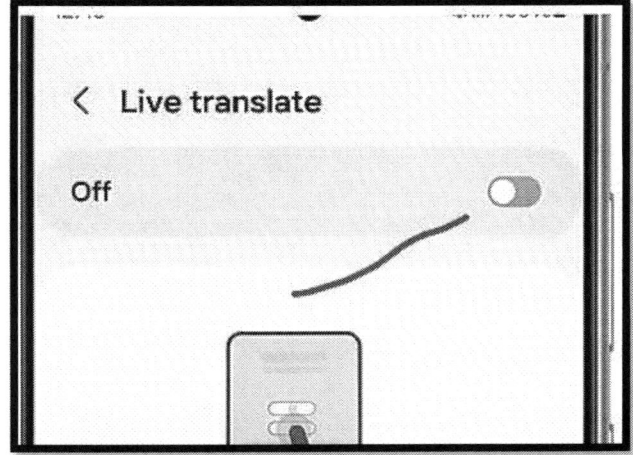

To enable live translation during a voice call, select **Call Assist > Live Translate.** On the translator panel at the top of the screen, choose the languages you want to use. Swipe right on the call screen and select **Stop translating** to end the translation. Open the Phone app, and select **More options > Settings > Live translate,** to make additional changes.

How to check voicemail

On the Samsung S24, the voicemail settings are quite simple to configure. These devices are produced to order and come equipped with a voicemail function already installed. This is very essential because it gives you the ability to send a voice message to anyone who is attempting to get in touch with you even when you are unable to answer your phone and take their calls. Calling the voicemail provider is the step that will allow you to configure the voicemail on your Galaxy S24 most quickly and easily. **This is simply like taking a shortcut, and if you want to give this strategy a try, the instructions are as follows:**

- Launch **the application with the keypad view** set as the default on the display.
- If you press and hold **the 1 key,** you will be connected to Voicemail right away.

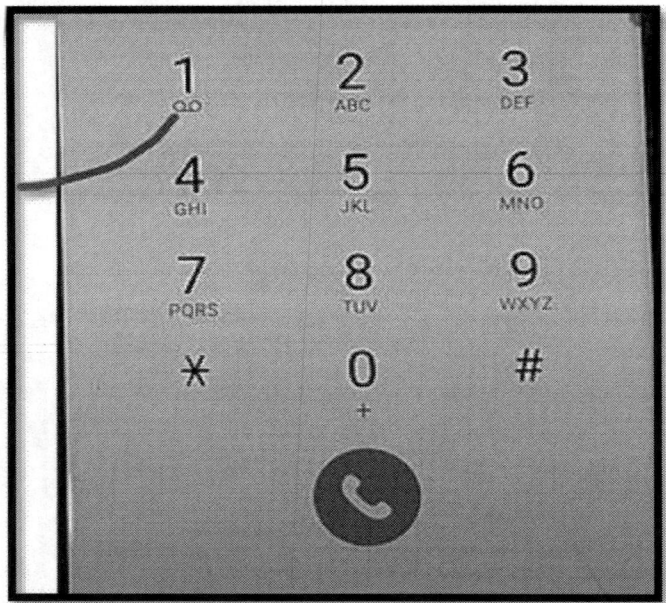

- You will be allowed to select your language of choice once the call has been connected.
- You will need to set up a voicemail password, which typically consists of anywhere from four to ten numbers if this is the first time you have set up this feature. However, if you have a voicemail box, you need to enter the password for the voicemail.
- You have the option of continuing to select the desired greeting or recording your greeting for your voicemail.

CHAPTER 5
CONTACTS APP

Create Contact

- Click to **open the Contacts app.**
- Choose a storage place.
- Enter your contact details and press **Save.**

Importing contacts

- You can add contacts to your device by bringing them from one of your other storage devices.
- Tap **Import contacts under Manage contacts > Options after launching the Contacts app.**

- To import contacts, adhere to the on-screen instructions.

Syncing contacts with your web accounts

Sync the contacts on your device with the contacts you've saved online in web accounts, like the Samsung account.

- To sync with an account, open Settings, select **Accounts and Backup > Manage accounts.**
- To enable Contacts, tap **Sync account and then tap the switch.**

Delete Contact

- Select **Options > Edit** after launching the Contacts app.
- Click **Delete** after selecting **Contacts.**

To eliminate a contact one at a time, select it from the contacts list, then select **More > Delete.**

Sharing contacts

By using different sharing options, you can share contacts with other people.

- Tap **Options > Edit after launching the Contacts app.**
- After choosing **contacts, click Share.**
- Decide on a sharing strategy.

Creating Groups

You can manage contacts by group and add groups, like friends or family.

- After launching the Contacts app, select **More > Groups > Create a group.**

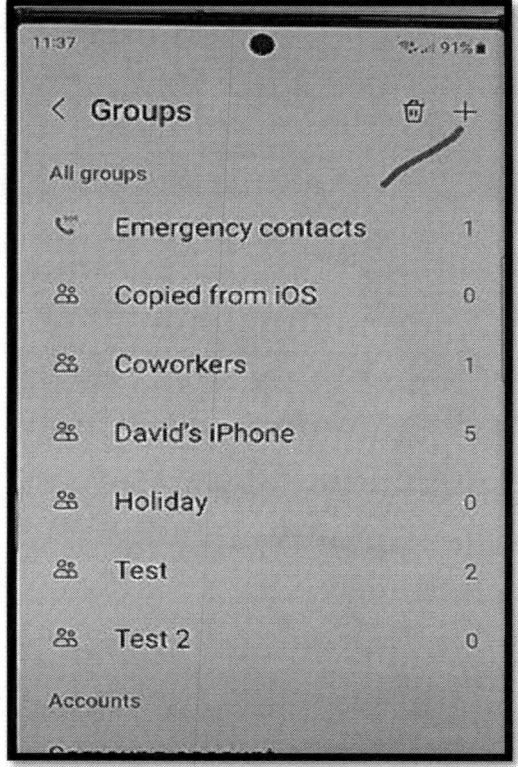

- To form a group, adhere to the instructions displayed on the screen.

Merging duplicate contacts

To make your contacts list more manageable, combine any duplicate contacts into a single contact.

- Launch the Contacts app, then select **More > Manage Contacts > Merge contacts.**
- Select contacts and press **Merg.**

Activity

1. Create a new contact.
2. Import contacts from your SIM card.
3. Synchronize your contact with your web accounts.
4. Delete contact; this can be contacts you do not need anymore.
5. Share contact from your phone to another.
6. Create a group of contacts on your phone.
7. Search for duplicate contacts on your phone and merge them.

CHAPTER 6

MESSAGES

With the use of the messaging app, you can transmit and receive messages based on dialogue. Sending and receiving messages while you are roaming may result in additional fees.

Send an SOS message

- Tap the New message icon when the Messages app is open.
- Once recipients are added, type a message.
  Simply touch, hold, and speak your message to send or record a voice message. The recording icon is only visible when there is nothing entered in the message field.
- Hit the send icon to send the message.

How can I Read the Messages I Receive?

You will get a notification in your messaging app when you have a message. To read this message, you must:

- Select **Messages** from the Samsung folder on the home screen, or swipe up to access your messaging app.

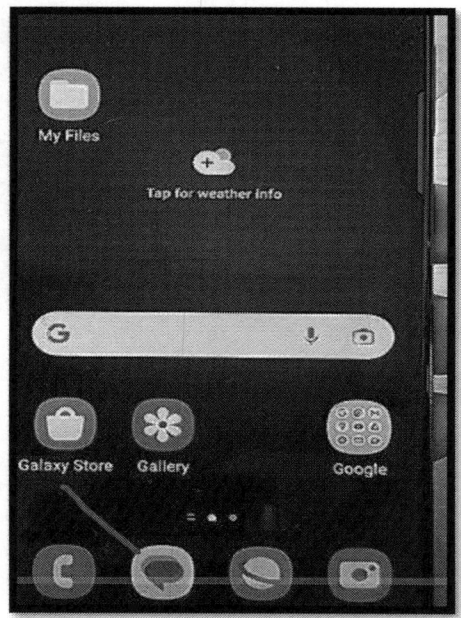

- A list of your conversations will appear when you first open the app. At the top of the list will be new messages; if a message is unread, a blue number (which represents the total number of unread messages in a conversation) will show up next to it.
- To view and read a message, tap **on it.**
- After reading the message, you have the option to respond by typing in the chat message box.
- After composing your message, click **the send symbol to send it.**

How to Know When Text Messages Have Been Read

You have the option to enable settings that will show you when your message has been read or delivered. To activate this:

- Launch **the messaging app.**
- Press **the menu icon (three dots).**
- Select **Settings.**
- Select **More settings.**
- Toggle between text and multimedia messages by tapping the one you want to use.
- To enable Show when delivered or Show when read, slide **the toggle.**
- "Delivered" will appear next to a text message once it has been delivered.
- A text message's status will indicate **"Read"** when it has been read.

Check Messages

- Select **Conversations after launching the Messages app.**

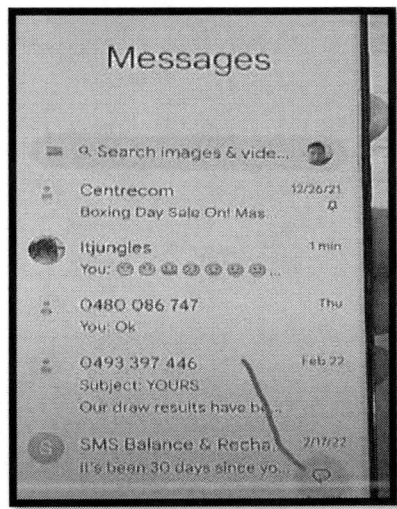

- Choose a contact or phone number from the messages list.
  - Tap the message input field, type a response and then **tap send to respond to the message.**

  - Pinch or spread two fingers apart on the screen to change the font size.

Sorting Messages

You can choose to get messages by making use of categories which is one of the easiest methods. Select Conversations after launching the Messages app.

To enable the category option if it is not visible, go to **More > Settings and select the Conversation categories switch.**

How to Forward the Message

The steps listed below will walk you through using your device's built-in forwarding feature.

- Select **Messages** from the Samsung folder on the home screen, or swipe up to access your apps.
- Click on **the message you want to send again.**
- A pop-up menu will appear if you tap and hold down on the message text.
- Press the **Forward button.**
- After making your selection(s), select Compose or Done. Go to step 6 if you don't see this screen.

- Click "**Send.**"

How to Add an Emoji to Your Message

With My Emoji, you can express yourself in entertaining and original ways. Make an emoji that resembles you! With My Emoji, you can take pictures and videos and share stickers with other people. Select Messages from the Samsung folder on the home screen, or swipe up to access your apps.

- Press the **symbol for Compose.**
- Tap the **Emoji icon on the Samsung keyboard**. To modify your keyboard settings, select the smiling face if you are unable to see this option.

- Select **the desired emoji to use.**

- Click **"Send."**

Please take note that using the built-in emoticons and smileys in a typical SMS (160 characters) shouldn't incur any fees. Emojis from a third-party keyboard have the potential to convert your SMS into an MMS, which, depending on the network, might cost money.

How to Delete a Message

- To delete a message, touch **and hold it, then select Delete.**

Message settings

- Tap **More > Settings** after launching the Messages app. Among other things, you can modify notification preferences and block unsolicited messages.

Activity

1. Send an emergency message on your phone.
2. Check your phone for new messages.
3. Forward a message you received to another contact on your phone.
4. Add an Emoji to a message you are about to send.
5. Delete a message from your message

CHAPTER 7
SETTINGS

In this chapter, you will learn about all of the various necessary settings needed for you to gain control of your device. Here you will learn how to tweak the display, lock screen settings, alter the screen mode, and lots more.

Display

Options

Modify the Home screen and the display. Press Display on the Settings screen and the following options will be made visible.

- **Light/Dark**: Enable or disable the Dark mode.
- **Dark mode settings**: When using the device at night or in a dimly lit area, reduce eye strain by turning on the dark theme. It is possible to schedule the application of Dark mode.
- **Brightness**: Modify the display's brightness.
- **Adaptive brightness**: Configure the gadget to remember your brightness settings and apply them automatically in comparable lighting environments.
- **Increased brightness**: Adjust the display's brightness beyond its highest setting. When you disable the adaptive brightness feature, this feature becomes available.
- **Motion smoothness**: Adjust the screen's refresh rate to achieve smoother motion. The screen will scroll more smoothly when the refresh rate is set high.
- **Eye comfort shield:** Lessen eye strain by preventing the screen from emitting too much blue light. This feature can be applied on a schedule.
- **Adaptive color tone**: To make colors seem more natural in various settings, modify the white balance and color palette according to the ambient lighting.
- **Full-screen apps**: Choose which applications to run in full-screen aspect ratio mode.
- **Camera cutout**: Configure the gadget to obscure the front camera on the display.
- **Screen timeout:** Configure the amount of time the gadget waits before turning off the backlight on the display.
- **Easy mode**: To see larger icons and a more straightforward layout on the Home screen, switch to the easy mode.
- **Edge panels:** Modify the Edge panel's configuration.
- **Navigator**: Modify the settings for the navigator.

- **Unintentional touch protection**: Configure the gadget to block touch input when it's in a dark area, like a pocket or purse.
- **Touch sensitivity:** To use screen protectors, turn up the screen's touch sensitivity.

Motion Smoothness

The number of times the screen is refreshed per second is known as the refresh rate. To stop the screen from flickering when switching between screens, use a high refresh rate. There will be a smoother screen scroll. A standard refresh rate allows you to get more use out of the battery.

- Select **Motion Smoothness under Display** on the Settings screen.

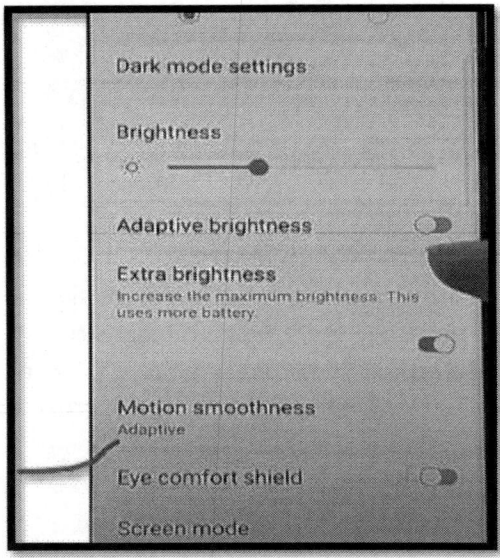

- Decide **on a refresh frequency.**
  - **Adaptive**: Increase the refresh rate of your screen automatically to get smoother scrolling and animations.
  - **Standard:** To save battery life, use a standard refresh rate in most circumstances.

Changing the screen mode or adjusting the display color

To suit your taste, you can change the display's color or screen mode.

Changing the screen mode

Choose your preferred mode by tapping Display > Screen mode on the Settings screen.

- **Vivid**: This maximizes your display's color saturation, sharpness, and range of colors. Additionally, you can change the color balance of the display by color value.
- **Natural**: This modifies the screen's tone to a more organic one.
    - The only mode where you can change the display's color is Vivid.
    - You might not be able to use third-party apps in vivid mode.

Optimizing the full screen color balance

Make your preferred color tone adjustments to get the best possible display color.

- Select **Display > Screen mode >**

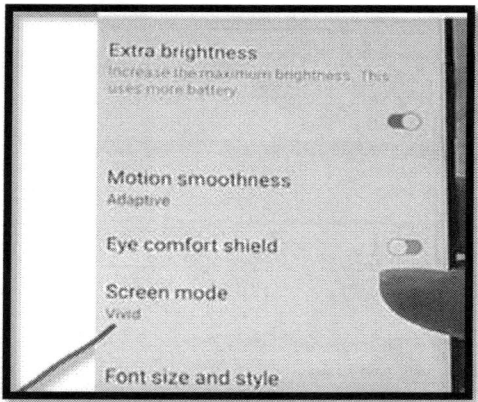

Vivid from the Settings screen, then play with the color adjustment bar under White balance.

The blue color tone will deepen as you move the color adjustment bar in the direction of Cool. The red color tone will intensify as you drag the bar in the direction of Warm.

Adjusting the tone of the screen with the use of color value

To adjust the intensity of a particular color tone, modify the values of Red, Green, and Blue separately.

- Select **Vivid under Display > Screen mode from the Settings screen**.
- Select **Advanced from the menu.**
- To suit your taste, reposition the G (Green), B (Blue), or R (Red) color bars. There will be a change in screen tone.

Wallpaper and Style / Themes

Modify the locked screen and the home screen's wallpaper. Toggle between **Wallpaper and Style on the Settings screen.** Change the Home screen, locked screen, and icon visuals on the device by applying different themes. Select **Themes from the Settings screen.**

Lock screen and AOD

The options available under this section include;

Modify the **Always On Display and Locked Screen settings**.

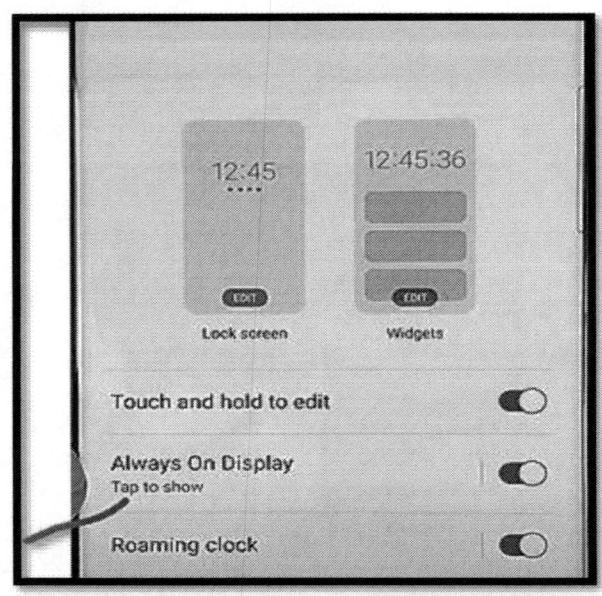

Select both the Lock screen and AOD from the Settings screen.

- **Type of screen lock**: Modify the screen lock technique.
- **Screen lock settings:** Adjust the screen lock settings for the chosen lock method to ensure security.
- **Touch and hold to edit:** To edit, touch and hold the locked screen to trigger the editing options to appear on the device.
- **Roaming clock**: When traveling, adjust the clock to display the home and local time zones on the secured screen.
- **Widgets:** Modify the parameters for the objects that show up when you tap the clock on a locked screen.
- **Regarding the Lock screen**: Review the Lock screen edition and legal details.

Extend Unlock

When trusted places or devices are detected, you can configure the device to automatically unlock and stay unlocked. For instance, if you designate your house as a trusted location, your device will recognize it when you arrive and unlock itself.

- To finish the setup, select **Lock screen and AOD > Extend Unlock from the Settings screen, then follow the on-screen directions.**
  - Once you've chosen a screen lock method, you can use this feature.
  - You must use the pattern, PIN, or password you set to unlock the screen when you turn on the device, or after four hours of non-use.

Always on Display (Displaying information when the screen is switched off)

When the screen is off, you can use it to view information, like the clock or calendar, or to control music playback. Moreover, you can check your notifications for any new calls or missed messages.

- On the Settings screen, tap **Lock screen and AOD > Always on Display > When to show, then choose your preferred option to limit the Always On Display's appearance to the predetermined condition.**

Opening notifications on the Always on Display

The Always on Display will show notification icons when you get missed calls, messages, or app alerts. To view a notification, double tap **on the icon.**

- To view notifications, you must unlock the screen if it is locked.

Turning off the Always on Display feature

To turn off the notification panel, open it, swipe down, and then tap (Always on Display). If the quick settings panel does not have (Always on Display), select **Edit and drag the button to add it.** As an alternative, you can disable AOD by tapping the **Always On Display switch after selecting Lock screen and AOD on the Settings screen.**

Internet

For your device, Samsung Internet is an easy-to-use, dependable, and speedy web browser.

Discover safer online browsing features that improve your browsing speed, safeguard your privacy, and make your online experience more enjoyable.

Browser tabs

To see multiple web pages at once, use tabs.

- Click **Tabs > New tab from the Internet.**
- Press **Tabs > Close tab to end a tab.**

Create a Bookmark

To easily access your favorite web pages, bookmark them.

- To save the open webpage, select **Add to bookmarks from the Internet.**

Open a Bookmark

Open a webpage quickly from the Bookmarks page.

- Select **Bookmarks** from the Internet.
- Select **an entry from your bookmark by tapping it.**

Save a webpage

Within the Samsung Internet app, there are multiple ways to store a webpage. **To access the following options, select Tools > Add page from the Internet.**

- **Bookmarks**: Include the website in your list of bookmarks.
- **Quick access:** See a list of frequently visited or bookmarked web pages.
- **Home screen**: On your Home screen, make a shortcut to the webpage.
- **Pages that are saved**: To access the webpage content offline, save its content to your device.

Secret mode

Viewed pages in secret mode don't appear in your search or browser history and don't leave any cookies or other traces on your device. Compared to regular tab windows, secret tabs are darker in color. Once you close the secret tab, any downloaded files stay on your device.

- Select **Tabs > Turn on Secret mode from the Internet.**
- To start browsing in secret mode, tap **Start.**

Secret mode settings

Use a biometric lock or password to access Secret mode.

- Select **Tabs from the Internet.**
- To access the following options, tap **More options > Secret mode settings:**
  - **Apply the password**: To use biometrics and enable Secret mode, create a password.
  - **Reset the secret mode**: Restore defaults and erase all of your data from the Secret mode.

Internet settings

Change the settings related to the Internet application.

- Hover over **Tools > Settings from the Internet.**

Activity

1. Make use of motion smoothness on your phone.
2. Change the screen mode and adjust the display color on your device.
3. Choose a wallpaper and theme of your choice.
4. With the use of the extend lock feature, lock your device.
5. Turn off the Always on Display feature.
6. With the use of the internet feature, browse the internet on your device.

CHAPTER 8

SOUND, VIBRATION & NOTIFICATION SETTINGS

Sound and Vibration Settings

Modify the device's settings to accommodate different sounds. Select **Sounds and Vibration from the Settings screen.**

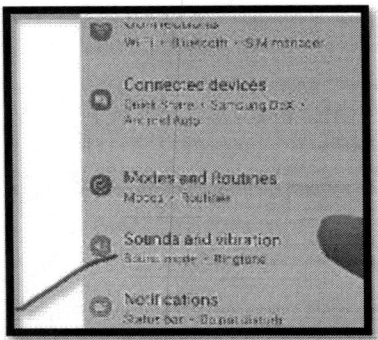

Below are the options available in these settings;

- **Mute, vibrate, or play music**: Select the device's sound, vibration, or silent modes.
- **Vibrate while ringing:** Play a ringtone for incoming calls and set the device to vibrate simultaneously.
- **Temporary mute:** Designate a specific amount of time for the device to be silent.
- **Ringtone:** Change the caller's ringtone.
- **Notification sound**: Modify the sound that is played.
- **System sound**: You can customize the sound for specific operations, like charging a device.
- **Volume**: Modify the volume on the gadget.
- **Call vibration:** Modify the vibrating call settings.
- **Notification vibration**: Modify the vibration alert configuration.
- **The vibration of the system:** Choose actions to modify the vibration's intensity and get feedback.
- **Vibration intensity**: Modify the vibration alert's power.

Vibrations

When and how your device vibrates is up to you.

- Select **Sounds and Vibration under Settings**.
- **To customize, tap options:**

- **Call vibration:** Select from pre-programmed call vibration patterns.
- **Vibration pattern selection for notifications:** Select from pre-programmed vibration patterns.
- **System vibration**: Set the following options' vibration intensity and feedback:
  - **Vibration intensity**: The vibration intensity of the system can be changed by dragging the slider.
  - **Touch interactions**: When you touch and hold items on the screen or tap **navigation buttons, the screen will vibrate**.
  - **Dialing keypad:** The phone keypad vibrates as you enter numbers.
  - **Samsung keyboard:** The Samsung keyboard vibrates as you type.
  - **Charging**: When a charger is plugged in, it vibrates.
  - **Gestures for navigation**: Shake when making a gesture.
  - **Camera feedback:** Vibrate when zooming, switching between shooting modes, and other operations.
- **Vibration intensity:** In this option, you can use the sliders to adjust the vibration intensity levels for calls, notifications, and touch interactions.

Volume

Adjust the volume of system sounds, media, call ringtones, and notifications.

- Drag the sliders for each type of sound by selecting **Sounds and Vibration > Volume from the Settings menu.**

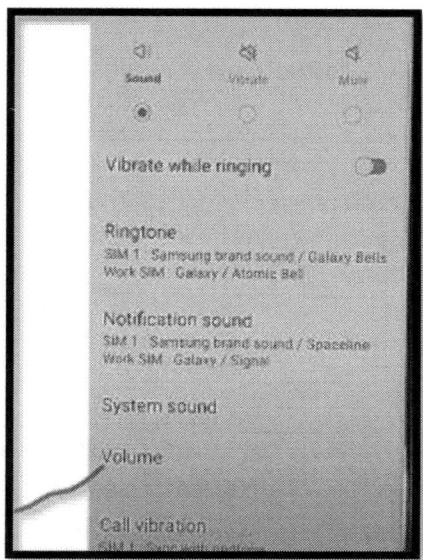

It should be noted that you can change the volume using the Volume keys as well. When pressed, the current sound type and volume level are displayed in a pop-up menu. After expanding the menu with a tap, you can drag the sliders for the other sound types to change their volume.

Using Volume keys for media

Change the default behavior of the Volume keys so that they control the media sound level instead of the active sound type.

- Select **Sounds and Vibration > Volume under Settings.**
- To activate this feature, choose **Use Volume keys for media.**

Media volume limit

Put a limit on the device's maximum volume output when using Bluetooth headphones or speakers.

- Select **Sounds and Vibration > Volume from the Settings menu.**
- Select **More options > Volume limit for media**.
- Press the toggle switch to make this feature active.
- Use the **Custom volume limit slider** to adjust the maximum output volume.
- To impose a PIN requirement on volume adjustments, select **Set volume limit PIN.**

Ringtone

On your Samsung Galaxy S24, changing the ringtone requires going into the sound settings and choosing a new one from a selection of pre-made call ringtones. Additionally, you have the option to add your sound. Note however that service providers may offer different options.

- Select **Sounds and Vibration > Ringtone from the Settings menu.**
- To change the volume of the ringtone, drag **the slider.**
- To use an audio file as a ringtone, tap **Add**; otherwise, tap **a ringtone** to hear a preview and select it.

Notification sound

Select a default sound to be used for all alerts.

- Select **Sounds and Vibration > Notification sound from the Settings menu**.
- To change the volume of the notification sound, drag **the slider.**
- To listen to a preview and choose it, tap **a sound.**

Using the App settings menu, you can also alter the notification sounds so that they are distinct for every app.

System sound

You can personalize the sounds on your device for different actions, such as charging and screen tapping. Service providers may offer different options.

- To access the following options, select **Sounds and Vibration > System sound from the Settings menu**:
    - **System sound volume**: To change the system volume, drag the slider.
    - **System sound theme**: Select a sound theme for the Samsung Keyboard, charging, touch interactions, and other features.
    - **Touch interactions**: In this option, when you tap or touch the screen to make a selection, sounds will play.
    - **Dialing keypad**: When entering numbers on the phone keypad, play a tone.
    - **Samsung keyboard:** When using the Samsung keyboard, make a sound.
    - **Charging**: Play a sound when the charger is plugged in.
    - **Screens lock/unlock**: When you lock or unlock the screen, a sound will be played.

Adapt sound

Tailor the sound to each ear to improve the quality of your listening.

- Select S**ettings and then press Sounds and Vibrations> Sound quality and effects >**

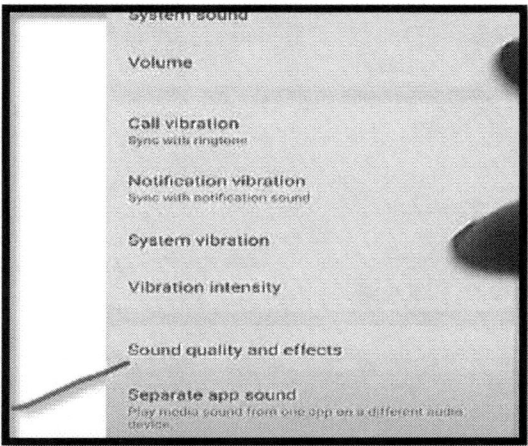

- **Adapt sound**.

- To choose when to adjust the sound settings, tap **Adapt Sound.**

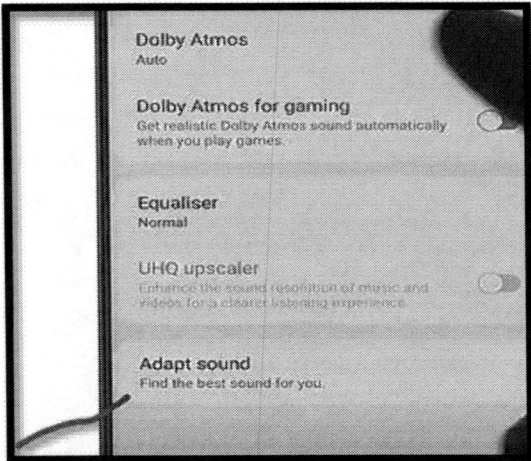

- To customize, tap **Settings** after selecting the sound profile that best suits your needs.

Press tests my hearing to help your device determine what sound is best for you.

Separate app sound

On a Bluetooth speaker or headset, you can set an app to play only media sound and turn off all other sounds (like notifications). This option appears in the Audio device menu only if you are connected to a Bluetooth device.

- Select **Sounds and Vibration > Separate app sound from the Settings menu.**
- After selecting **Turn on Now** to activate the Separate app sound, adjust the following settings:
    - **App**: Select an application to stream its audio to a different audio device.
    - **Audio device**: Select the audio device on which you wish to play the sound from the app.

Notification Settings

You can personalize your Samsung Galaxy S24's notification settings to receive alerts about a range of events, including incoming calls, messages, app notifications, and more. App alerts can be prioritized and streamlined by customizing which apps send notifications and how you are alerted.

App notifications

Select the applications that are permitted to notify you.

- To enable notifications for specific apps, navigate to **Notifications > App notifications from the Settings menu.**

Do not disturb

You can disable notifications and sounds when the "Do not disturb" mode is activated. It's also possible to designate exceptions for alarms, people, and apps. It is also possible to schedule regular activities such as meetings or sleep. To configure the following, select **Notifications > Do not disturb from the Settings menu.**

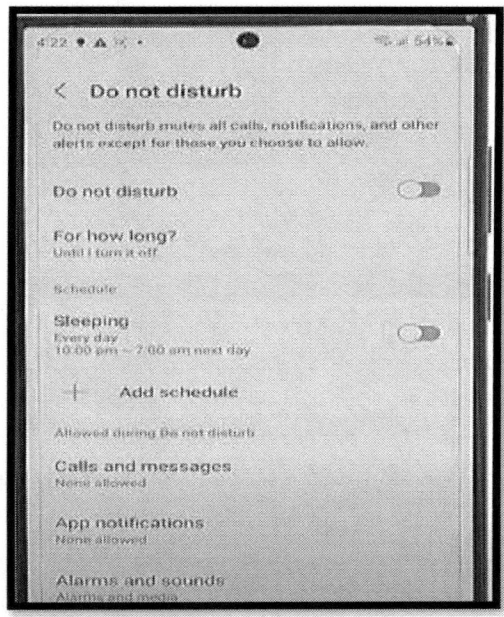

- **Don't disturb**: To disable notifications and sounds, select **Do Not Disturb.**
- **How much time will it last?**: When you manually activate Do Not Disturb mode, you can specify its default duration.
  - **Schedule**
    - **Sleeping:** While you sleep, create a personalized routine for the "Do Not Disturb" mode.
    - **Add the timetable:** Make a new schedule that specifies the days and times that you should routinely place your device in "do not disturb" mode.
  - **Allowed during Do not disturb**
  - **Messages and calls:** Allow **Do Not Disturb** Exceptions by tapping it.

- o **Notifications from apps**: Add the apps you want to be alerted from when in do-not-disturb mode. Even if you deny permission for the related apps, you will still receive calls, messages, and conversation notifications.
- o **Sound and vibration alerts:** While the "Do not disturb" mode is in effect, turn on sound and vibration alerts for events, alarms, and reminders.
- o **Hide notifications**: To hide notifications, view the customization options.

Sound quality and effects

Adjust the sound quality and effects on the device.

- Select **Sounds and Vibration> Sound quality and effects** from the Settings screen.
- **Dolby Atmos**: Choose a surround sound mode with Dolby Atmos that is best suited for different kinds of audio, including music, movies, and voice. You can experience flowing, moving audio sounds all around you when you use Dolby Atmos.
- **Dolby Atmos for gaming**: Play games with Dolby Atmos sound optimized for an immersive gaming experience.
- **Equalizer**: Choose a setting to enjoy optimized sound for a particular genre of music.
- **UHQ Upscaler**: When using wired headphones, improve the sound quality of music and videos.
- **Adapt sound**: Adjust the sound to what works best for you.

Dolby Atmos

The goal of Dolby Atmos, an advanced sound technology created by Dolby Laboratories, is to deliver an immersive audio experience for a variety of entertainment mediums, such as video games, music, and movies. In contrast to conventional surround sound systems that rely on channels, Dolby Atmos introduces the idea of overhead speakers and audio objects to produce an audio environment that is more dynamic and three-dimensional.

- To access the following options, navigate to **Sounds and Vibration > Sound Quality and Effects from the Settings menu.**
  - **Dolby Atmos**: Experience cutting-edge audio that surrounds and rises above you with Dolby Atmos.
  - **Dolby Atmos for gaming**: here you can make use of Dolby Atmos which has been optimized for gaming.

Equalizer

An audio signal's frequency balance can be altered with the use of an equalizer (EQ), a tool, or a gadget. Users can fine-tune the sound to suit their preferences or optimize it for various types of audio content by controlling the volume levels of specific frequency bands. Equalizers are frequently found in home theater systems, software programs, and audio equipment. There is an equalizer built into your S24 so you can adjust the sound profile to your liking. By adjusting various frequency bands, the equalizer lets you maximize the audio output for your speakers or headphones by amplifying or decreasing particular audio frequencies.

- Select **Sounds and Vibration > Sound quality and effects from the Settings menu.**
- To select a genre of music, tap **Equalizer.**

UHQ upscaler

This feature improves the audio quality of films and music to enjoy a more lucid auditory experience. This function can only be accessed when a headset is connected.

- Selec**t Sounds and Vibration> Sound Quality and Effects from the Settings menu.**
- Select an upscaling option by tapping **UHQ upscale.**

Activity

1. Adjust the sound and vibration settings on your phone.
2. Set a ringtone on your device.
3. Adjust the volume of notifications on your device.
4. Adjust sound quality and effects with the use of the equalizer.
5. Activate "Do Not Disturb" if you need it.

CHAPTER 9

CONNECTION SETTINGS

You will discover how to personalize the device settings in this chapter. To get started,

- Select **Settings from the Apps screen. As an alternative, swipe to reveal the notification panel.**

Press the **search icon** to search for settings using keywords. By choosing a tag under Suggestions, you can also search for settings.

Wi-Fi

To access the internet or other network devices, turn on the Wi-Fi feature and connect to a Wi-Fi network.

Connecting to a Wi-Fi network

- To activate Wi-Fi, go to **Connections**

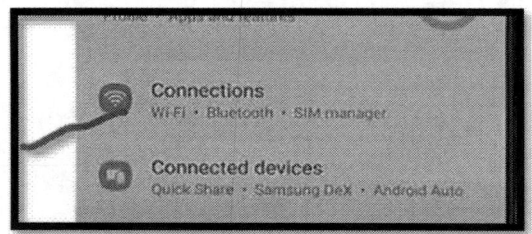

> **Wi-Fi on the Settings screen,**

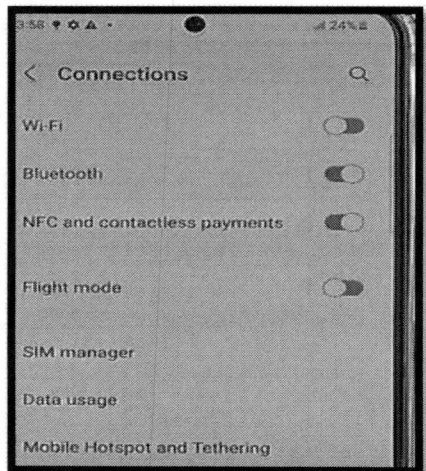

Then tap the switch.

From the list of Wi-Fi networks, choose a network. It is worth noting that passwords are needed for networks that have a lock icon. **Take the following into consideration;**

- Without a password, the device will automatically reconnect to a Wi-Fi network once it has established a connection. Turn off the **Auto-reconnect feature by tapping the switch next to the network to stop the device from connecting to it automatically.**
- Try restarting the wireless router or the Wi-Fi feature on your device if you are having trouble connecting to a network.

Checking out the Wi-Fi network quality information

Examine the Wi-Fi network quality metrics, including stability and speed.

- To activate Wi-Fi, go to **Connections > Wi-Fi on the Settings screen**, then tap the **switch.** The Wi-Fi networks will have the network quality information displayed underneath them. To enable it if it is not visible, select **More options > Intelligent Wi-Fi and then tap the Show network quality info switch.**

Sharing Wi-Fi network passwords

You can connect to a secured Wi-Fi network without entering the password if you ask someone who is already connected to share it with you. This feature can only be used between devices that are in contact with one another, and the other device's screen needs to be turned on.

- To enable Wi-Fi, navigate to **Connections > Wi-Fi on the Settings screen and press the switch.**
- From the list of Wi-Fi networks, **choose a network.**

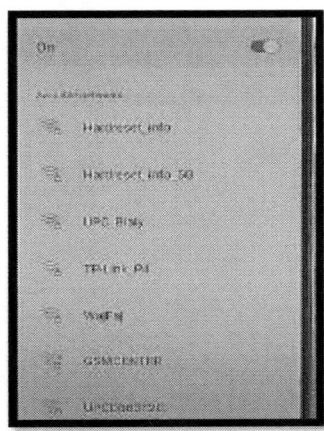

- Click **Password Request.**

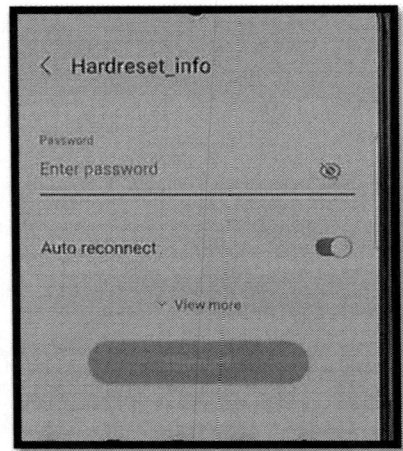

- On the other device, **accept the share request.** Your device has successfully entered the Wi-Fi password and is now connected to the network.

Wi-Fi Direct

With Wi-Fi Direct, devices can connect to a Wi-Fi network directly without the need for an access point.

- To activate Wi-Fi, go to **Connections > Wi-Fi on the Settings screen, then tap the switch.**
- Select **Wi-Fi Direct under More**. A list of the detected devices is provided.
- Ask the device to activate its Wi-Fi Direct feature if the one you wish to connect to is not on the list.
- To connect to a device, choose anyone of your choice. When the other device approves the Wi-Fi Direct connection request, the devices will be linked. Choose the **device to disconnect from the list to break the connection.**

Bluetooth

To transfer media files or data between devices that support Bluetooth, use Bluetooth.

Below are certain precautions for the use of Bluetooth;

- Samsung disclaims all liability for mishandling, loss, or interception of data transmitted or received via Bluetooth.
- Make sure that any device you share or receive data from has been properly secured and is trustworthy. The operating distance may be shortened if there are obstructions between the devices.

- It's possible that some gadgets won't work with yours, particularly ones that the Bluetooth SIG hasn't tested or approved.
- Avoid using the Bluetooth feature for nefarious activities, such as file piracy or intercepting communications without authorization for profit. The consequences of using the Bluetooth feature illegally are not Samsung's fault.

Pairing with other Bluetooth devices

- To enable Bluetooth, navigate to **Connections > Bluetooth on the Settings screen**, then press **the switch**. A list of the detected devices will appear.

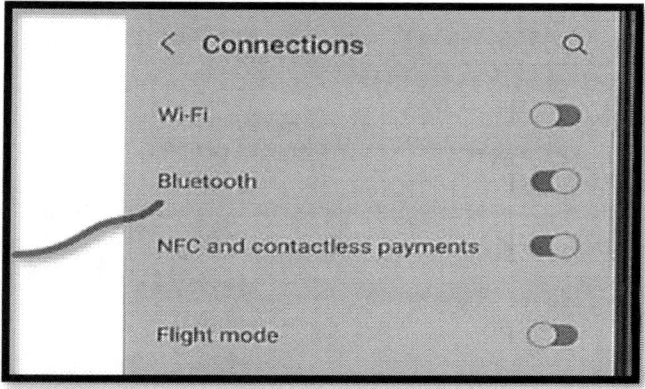

- To pair with a device, choose one. Put the device into Bluetooth pairing mode if the one you wish to pair with is not on the list. Consult the user manuals for the other device. When the Bluetooth settings screen is open, other devices can see your phone.
- To confirm, grant the Bluetooth connection request on your phone.
  When the other device accepts the Bluetooth connection request, the devices will be linked.
  To disconnect the devices, select **Settings next to the name of the device, then select Unpair.**

Sending and receiving data

- Launch **the Gallery app, and then choose a picture.**
- To send the image to a device, tap the **Share icon > Bluetooth** and choose the specific device.
  Ask the device to activate its visibility feature if the one you wish to pair with isn't on the list.
- Grant the other device's request for a Bluetooth connection.

NFC and Contactless payments

Near field communications tags (NFC) are tags with product information that you can read with your phone. Once the necessary apps have been downloaded, you can use this feature to pay for purchases and to purchase tickets for events or transportation. Your S24 has an integrated NFC antenna. To prevent harming the NFC antenna, handle it with caution.

Reading information from NFC tags

To read product information from NFC tags, use the NFC feature.

- To enable NFC and contactless payments, go to the **Settings screen, select Connections, and then tap the NFC and contactless payments switch.**
- Position your device's NFC antenna area on the back near an NFC tag. The data from the tag is displayed.

For the device to read NFC tags and receive data, make sure the screen is turned on and unlocked.

Making payments with the NFC feature

Registration for the mobile payment service is required before you can use the NFC feature to make payments. Get in touch with your service provider to sign up or for additional details about the program.

- To enable contactless payments and NFC, navigate to the **Connections screen from the Settings screen and tap the switch.**
- To use the NFC card reader, simply touch the NFC antenna area on the back of your device.

Open the Settings screen, select **Connections > NFC and contactless payments > Contactless payments > Payment**, and then choose an app to set as the default payment app. Not all of the available payment apps may be included in the list of payment services. It is possible that the payment services you previously used won't function correctly if you update the app or install a new one. In that scenario, choose another app from the list of installed or updated apps by tapping **Connections > NFC and contactless payments > Contactless payments > Payment or Others on the Settings screen. Alternately, deselect the chosen app.**

Data usage

The quantity of data used by a device to connect to the internet or exchange information with other devices over a network is referred to as data usage. This information may be presented as emails, texts, pictures, videos, app updates, or other kinds of material. It's critical to comprehend and control data usage, particularly for users with data plans that are limited or when utilizing mobile networks that have extra fees.

- Click on **Connections > Data usage from Settings**.

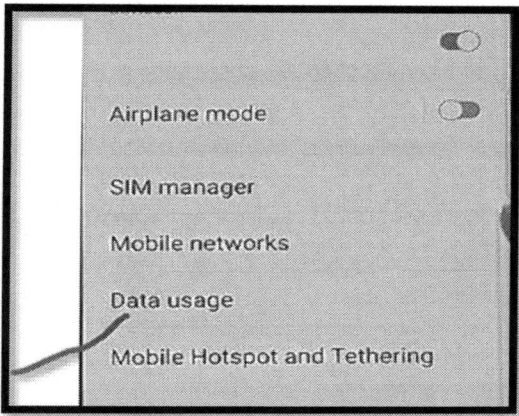

Turn on Data Saver

To cut down on data usage, use Data Saver, which stops certain apps from sending or receiving data in the background.

- Select **Connections > Data usage > Data saver** from the Settings menu.

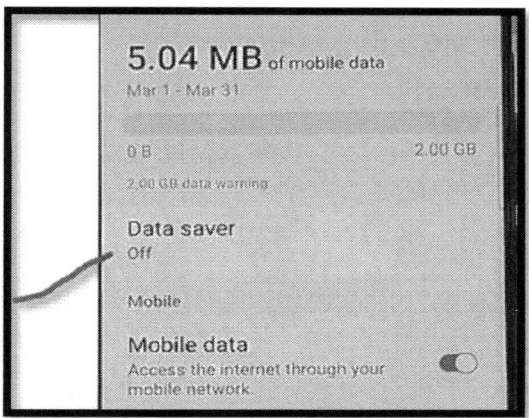

- To activate **Data Saver, tap it.**
  - Select **Allowed** using data while Data saver is on to give some apps unrestricted data usage, and select the app's restrictions by tapping next to it.

More connection settings

To regulate additional connection features, modify the settings.

- Select **Connections > More connection settings from the Settings screen.**
- Configure your phone to look for nearby devices so you can connect to them.
- **Printing:** Adjust the parameters for the device's installed printer plug-ins. To print files, you can manually add a printer or search for available ones. For additional information, see Printing.
- **VPN**: To access a private network at a business or school, set up a virtual private network (VPN) on your device.
- **Private DNS**: Configure the device to use the enhanced security private DNS.
- **Ethernet**: You can use a wired network and adjust network settings when you connect an Ethernet adapter.

Virtual Private Networks

A technology known as a virtual private network, or VPN, establishes a secure, encrypted connection over a less secure network, like the Internet. VPNs are frequently used to improve security and privacy when connecting to a private network from a remote location, accessing sensitive data, or browsing the internet. Your internet traffic is routed through a VPN server situated in a particular location when you connect to a VPN. Websites and online services see the IP address of the VPN server while your real IP address is hidden.

- Select **Connections > More connection settings >**

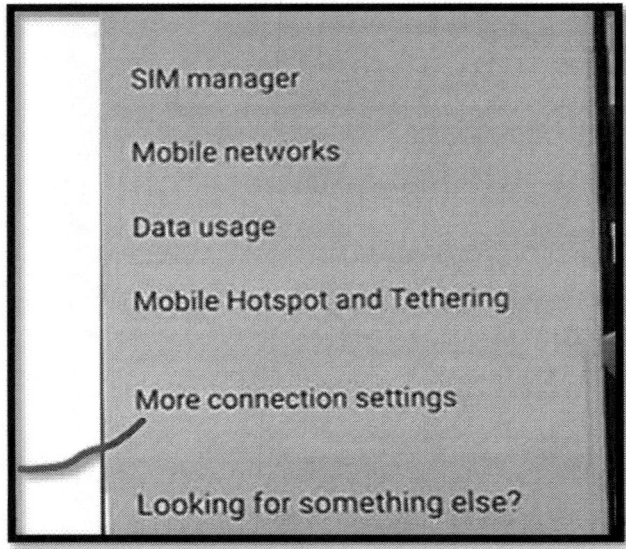

VPN from the Settings menu

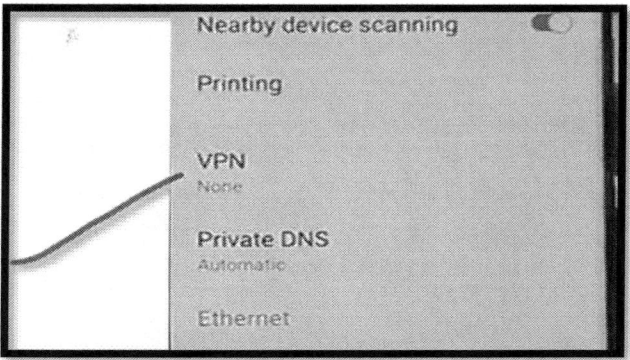

- Select **More Choices** > **Add a VPN profile.**

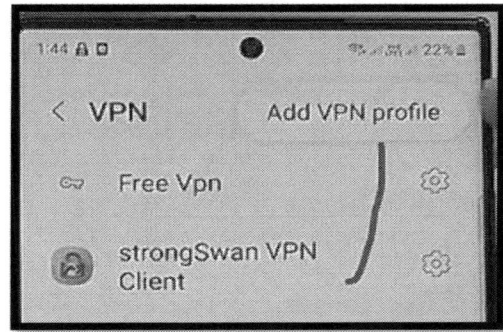

- After entering the VPN network details that your network administrator has provided, click **Save.**

Manage a VPN

To change or remove a VPN connection, use the VPN settings menu.

- Select **Connections** > **More connection settings** > **VPN from the Settings menu.**
- When a VPN appears, tap **Settings.**
- To make changes to the VPN, select **Save**, or to remove it, select **Delete.**

Connect to a VPN

It's simple to connect to and disconnect from a VPN once it's set up.

- Select **Connections** > **More connection settings** > **VPN from the Settings menu**.
- Select a VPN, input your login details, and then select **Connect.**
- Tap the VPN, and then select **Disconnect to end the connection.**

Ethernet

If a wireless network connection is unavailable, you can link your device to a local network using an Ethernet cable.

- Link your device to an Ethernet cable.
- Select **Connections > More connection settings > Ethernet from the Settings menu**, then adhere to the instructions.

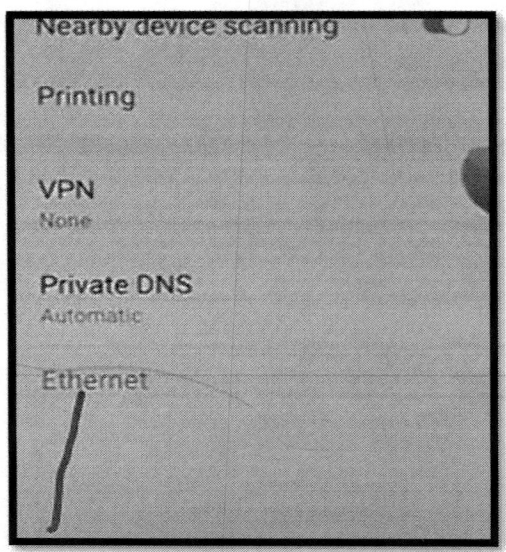

Mobile hotspot

To share your phone's mobile data connection with other devices, use it as a mobile hotspot.

- Select **Connections > Mobile Hotspot and Tethering > Mobile Hotspot from the Settings screen.**
- To turn it on, just tap the switch. In addition to the password, you can modify the network name. The status bar will display the icon.
- Go to the Wi-Fi networks list on the other device, find your phone, and pick it up. As an alternative, scan the **QR code with the other device by tapping it on the Mobile Hotspot screen.**
    - On your phone, set Band to 2.4 GHz, select Advanced, and then tap the Hidden network switch to turn it off if the mobile hotspot is not detected.
    - You can share the mobile data connection on your phone with other devices that are signed into your Samsung account if you enable the Auto Hotspot feature.

Printing

Set up the printer plug-ins that is installed on the device. Images and documents can be printed by connecting the device via Wi-Fi or Wi-Fi Direct to a printer. It's possible that some printers won't work with your device.

For the printers you wish to use the device with, add printer plug-ins by doing the following;

- Select **Connections > More connection settings > Printing > Download plugin from the Settings screen.**
- Choose and install **a printer by plugging it in.**
- Choose the printer plug-in that is installed. When it comes to printers, the device will automatically look for ones that are linked to the same wireless network as it.
- Choose a printer to get it added. To add printers manually, choose **More options > Add printer.**

Connected devices

Modify the device connection settings. Select Connected Devices from the Settings screen.

Quick Share: Modify the Quick Share configuration.
Music Share: Modify the Music Share configuration.
Auto-switch Buds: You can program the Galaxy Buds to automatically switch between your phone and another device when you play media, make or receive calls, and more. Only when you are wearing your Galaxy Buds and have logged into the same Samsung account on the other device is this feature available to you.
Call and text on other devices: By connecting your phone and tablet, you can utilize the tablet's messaging and calling capabilities along with your phone number. On the tablet and phone, you have to create an account and log in with the same Samsung credentials. It's possible that some messaging and calling features won't work.

- **Continue using the apps on different devices**: Utilize the apps on your phone on other devices that are linked to your Samsung account.
- **Camera sharing**: Share your phone's camera with a neighboring tablet or Galaxy Book by using its camera as a webcam. To utilize this feature, Wi-Fi, Bluetooth, and the Camera sharing feature must all be enabled on both devices and they must be signed into the same Samsung account.
- **Link to Windows**: Using a Windows computer, access and utilize the data from the mobile device, including apps and images.
- **Multi-control:** Utilize a Samsung computer that supports this feature on your phone along with a mouse and keyboard.

- **Samsung DeX**: Utilize the capabilities of your smartphone in a computer-like interface.
- **Smart View**: Connect your phone to a TV or monitor that supports screen mirroring to view the content it has displayed on a larger screen.
- **Galaxy Wearable**: You can personalize the wearable device's settings and apps by connecting it to your phone.
- **SmartThings:** Manage and operate Internet of Things (IoT) devices and smart appliances.
- **Android Auto**: Link your gadget to a car and use the dashboard to operate certain of your device's functions.

Modes and Routines

To make use of your device more conveniently, choose a mode based on what you're doing or where you are. You can also set up routines for your frequent usage patterns. Navigate to the **Modes and Routines screen in Settings.**

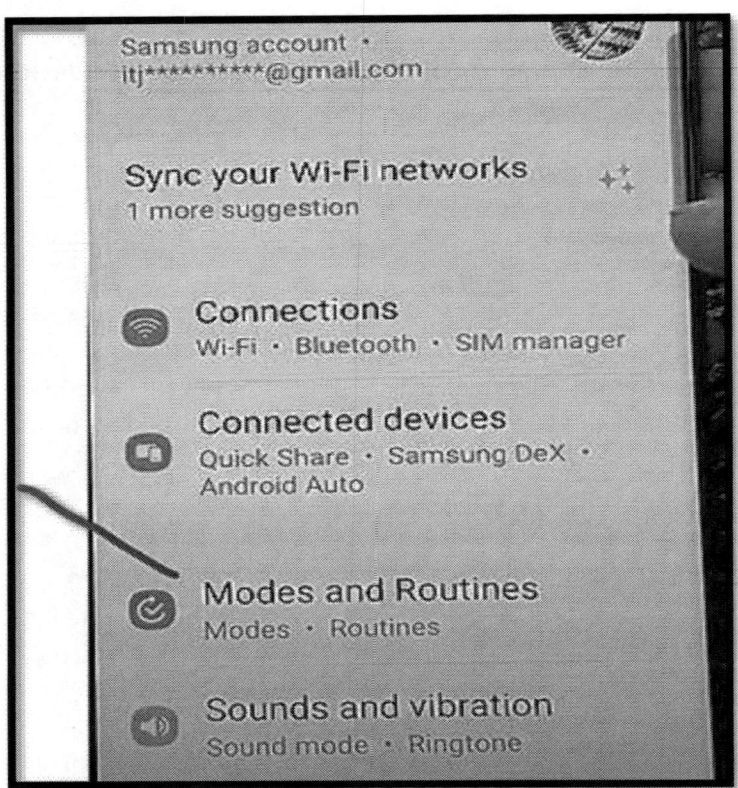

Adding modes

- Touch **Modes underneath Modes and Routines** when you access the settings screen.
- Touch **Add mode** to include a mode of your choice.

Running modes

You can choose to run modes manually by tapping the button whenever you want, or you can run them automatically when their conditions are detected.

- To run a mode manually, select **it and tap Turn on.**
- To stop a running mode, tap **the mode and tap Turn off.**

Adding routines

- Select **Modes and Routines > Routines from the Settings screen.**
- To add your routines, tap **the add icon to include a routine of your own, or tap and select a desired routine.**
  Click **Start manually** to change the routine's running condition to manual. Only in the absence of any configured running conditions will this option be visible.

Running routines

When their conditions are identified, auto routines will begin to execute automatically. You can manually run routines that you have set to run with the running condition set to start manually by tapping the button whenever you choose. Tap **the button next to the routine** you wish to execute by hand. To utilize a widget, select **a routine from the Manual routines list**, then select **More > Set as widget > Add.** You can launch the routine by tapping the widget, which will be added to the Home screen as a widget. Routines can be stopped by tapping **the one under Running and selecting Stop.**

Activity

1. Connect your phone to a Wi-Fi connection.
2. With the use of Bluetooth, send a document or file from your phone to another.
3. With the use of the data saver feature, save the amount of data you consume on your device.
4. Explain what Virtual Private Networks are.
5. Turn on your mobile hotspot and get other phones connected to your device.
6. What are Modes and Routines and what are their functions?

CHAPTER 10

LOCK SCREEN, BIOMETRICS, AND SECURITY

In this chapter, you will learn how to verify and adjust the device's privacy and security settings.

- Select **Security and Privacy from the Settings screen.**

Below are some of the options available under security and privacy;

- **Lock screen**: Modify the locked screen's configuration.
- **Account security:** Modify your accounts' settings.
- **Lost device protection**: Protect your lost device by turning on or off the Find My Mobile feature. Go to smartthingsfind.samsung.com to monitor and manage your misplaced or pilfered phone. Additionally, you can use this phone to see where the wearable gadgets are located.
- **App security:** Protect your device from harmful software by scanning apps.
- **Updates**: Verify the software version of your device and look for updates.
- **Biometrics:** Modify the biometric data settings.
- **Auto Blocker:** Protect your gadget by preventing threats and other dubious activity from accessing it.
- **Additional security settings**: Set up extra security.
- **Permissions utilized in the last 24 hours**: Examine the permission usage history of the app or feature.
- **Permission manager:** Manage your device's permissions to grant or deny apps access to specific features or data.
- **Extra privacy controls**: Limit who can use the clipboard and microphone, for example.
- **Additional privacy settings**: Set up extra privacy preferences.

Lock screen

When the **Side button** is pressed, the screen locks and turns off. Additionally, if the device is not used for a predetermined amount of time, the screen automatically locks and turns off.

- When the screen turns on, swipe in any direction to unlock it. Hit the **Side button or double-tap the screen to turn it on or off, respectively.**

Edit shortcuts

The shortcuts to different apps or features can be changed at the bottom of the locked screen.

- When the screen is locked, touch and hold it, tap the shortcut icon, choose the **desired app or feature, and finally tap Done.**

Changing the screen lock method

- Open **Settings**, select **Screen lock type > AOD > Lock screen,** and then choose a different screen lock method.

Your personal information is protected when you use a screen lock method that requires you to set a pattern, PIN, password, or biometric data to keep others from accessing your device. The device will require an unlock code to be unlocked after the screen lock method is set. If you put in the unlock code incorrectly multiple times in a row and exceed the number of attempts, you have the option to force a factory data reset on your device.

- Navigate to Settings, select **Lock screen and AOD > Secure lock settings**, use the preset screen lock method to unlock the screen, and then select the **Auto factory** reset switch to activate it.

Face recognition

The device has the option to recognize your face to unlock the screen.

When using this option, take note of the following;

- The first time you unlock the screen after turning on the device, you will not be able to use your face as a screen lock method. You must use the pattern, PIN, or password you set when registering the face to unlock the screen to use the device. Take care not to lose track of your password, PIN, or pattern.
- All of your biometric information will be erased if you choose the less secure screen lock options of **Swipe or None.**

Precautions for using face recognition

Take note of these safety measures before using your device's face recognition feature.

- Someone or something that resembles you could unlock your device.
- Compared to passwords, PINs, and patterns, face recognition is less secure.

For better face recognition

When using face recognition, take into account the following:

- When registering, take into account any requirements, such as donning masks, hats, glasses, beards, or excessive makeup.
- When registering, make sure the camera lens is clean and that you are in a well-lit area.
- Make sure your photo is clear for optimal matching outcomes.

Registering your face

Register your face inside and away from the sun for optimal face registration.

- Select **Security and Privacy**

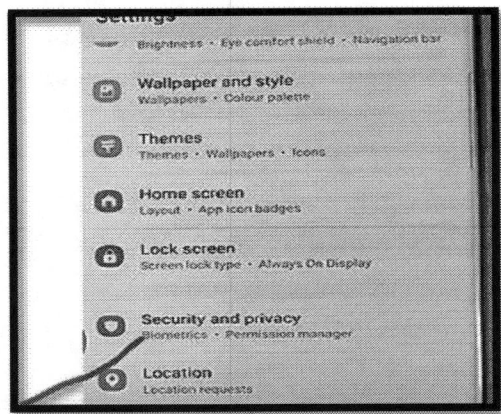

> Biometrics

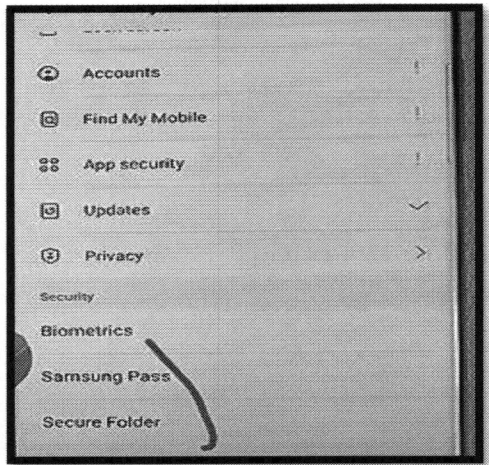

> Face Recognition from the Settings screen.

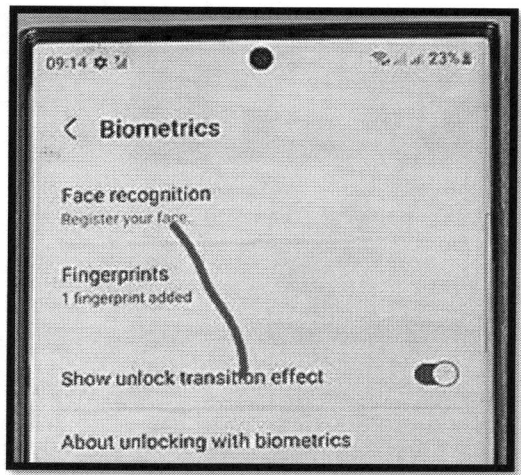

- After reading the instructions on the screen, click **Continue**.
- Choose **a screen lock technique.**
- Place your face within the screen's frame. The camera will look at your face.
  - If using your face to unlock the screen isn't working properly, you can register your face again by removing it by tapping Remove face data.
  - You can add an alternate appearance and improve face recognition by tapping Add alternative appearance.

Unlocking the screen with your face

Rather than utilizing a pattern, PIN, or password to unlock the screen, you can do it with your face.

- Select **Security and Privacy > Biometrics > Face Recognition from the Settings screen.**
- Use the preset screen lock method to unlock the screen.
- To activate it, simply tap **the Face unlock switch.**
- Examine the screen on the locked screen. You don't need to use any additional screen lock methods once your face is recognized. Use the preset screen lock method if your face does not appear to be recognized.

Deleting the registered face data

You have the option to remove your registered face data.

- Select **Security and Privacy> Biometrics > Face Recognition from the Settings screen.**
- Use the preset screen lock method to unlock the screen.

- Press **Remove face data > Remove**. All associated features will be disabled upon deletion of the registered face.

Fingerprint Recognition

Your device must register and store your fingerprint information for fingerprint recognition to work. **Please take note of the following as regards the use of fingerprints on your device**

- This feature might not be accessible based on the model or carrier.
- Fingerprint recognition improves device security by utilizing each fingerprint's distinctive qualities. There is very little chance that the fingerprint sensor will confuse two distinct fingerprints. Nonetheless, the sensor might identify two fingerprints as identical in rare instances where they are strikingly similar.
- Performance may be impacted by thick protective film. Make sure the screen protector you use is labeled as compatible with the on-screen fingerprint sensor if you use one.
- (As in the Samsung screen protectors that are sold)
- When you turn on the device, you won't be able to use your fingerprint to unlock the screen for the first time if you use a screen lock. You have to use the pattern, PIN, or password you set when registering the fingerprint to unlock the screen to use the device. Take care not to lose track of your password, PIN, or pattern.
- Re-register your fingerprints if yours isn't recognized, and then use the pattern, PIN, or password you set when registering the fingerprint to unlock the device. You will not be able to use the device if you do not reset it if you forget your pattern, PIN, or password. Forgotten unlock codes can cause data loss or inconvenience, but Samsung is not liable for either.
- All of your biometric information will be erased if you choose the less secure screen lock options of Swipe or None.

For better fingerprint recognition

The following circumstances could impact the functionality of the feature when you scan your fingerprint on the device:

- Uneven or scarred fingerprints might not be recognized by the device.
- Small or thin fingers' fingerprints might not be recognized by the device.
- Register the fingerprints of the fingers you use most frequently to operate the device to enhance recognition performance.
- A fingerprint recognition sensor is integrated into the bottom center of your device. Make sure that nothing sharp, like coins, keys, pens, or necklaces,

scratches, or damages the screen protector or the screen on the fingerprint recognition sensor area.

- Make sure your fingers are dry and clean, as well as the fingerprint recognition sensor area located in the bottom center of the screen.
- Your fingerprints might not be recognized by the device if you use a fingertip or bend your finger. Press the screen until your fingertip covers the entire area designated for fingerprint recognition.

Registering fingerprints

- To register your fingerprint, navigate to **Security and Privacy > Biometrics > Fingerprints on the Settings screen**,

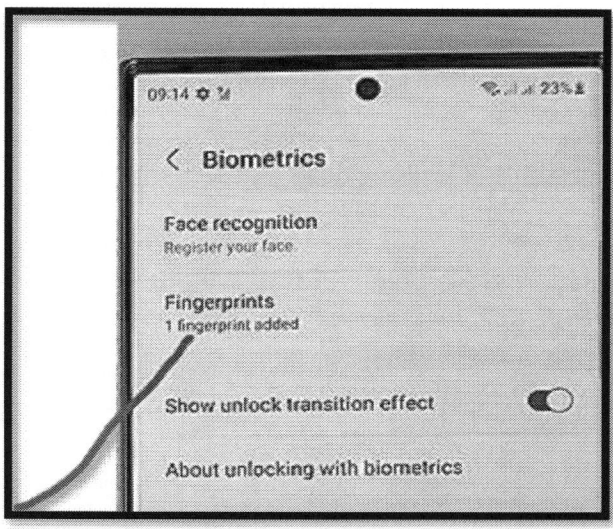

Then follow the prompts on the screen. By selecting **Check added fingerprints after registering, you can verify if your fingerprint has been registered and what its name is.**

Unlocking the screen with your fingerprints

Using your fingerprint, rather than a pattern, PIN, or password, you can unlock the screen.

- Select **Security and Privacy> Biometrics > Fingerprints from the Settings screen.**
- Use the preset screen lock method to unlock the screen.
- To activate it, simply tap **the fingerprint unlock switch.**
- Slide your finger over the fingerprint recognition sensor on the locked screen to have your fingerprint scanned.

Recognizing your fingerprints with the screen turned off

- You can access Fingerprints under **Settings > Security and Privacy > Biometrics**.
- Employing the preset screen lock method, unlock the screen.
- You can activate it by tapping the Fingerprint always on the switch. You can adjust when the fingerprint recognition icon appears or opt not to see it at all by tapping the **Show icon when the screen button is off.**

Deleting registered fingerprints

Fingerprints that are registered can be removed.

- Select **Security and Privacy > Biometrics > Fingerprints from the Settings screen.**
- Use the preset screen lock method to unlock the screen.
- To remove a fingerprint, select it and press **Remove.**

Find My Mobile

Users can remotely locate, track, and manage their Samsung smartphones or tablets with the "Find My Mobile" feature. The service provides many features, including data backup, device locking, and device location, which can be helpful in various situations. By enabling remote data deletion, online tracking, and locking features, you can guard your device against theft or loss. Note also that using Find My Mobile requires having a Samsung account and having Google location service enabled.

Turn on Find My Mobile

You have to activate and personalize the Find My Mobile feature before you can use it.

- Select **Security and Privacy > Find My Mobile**

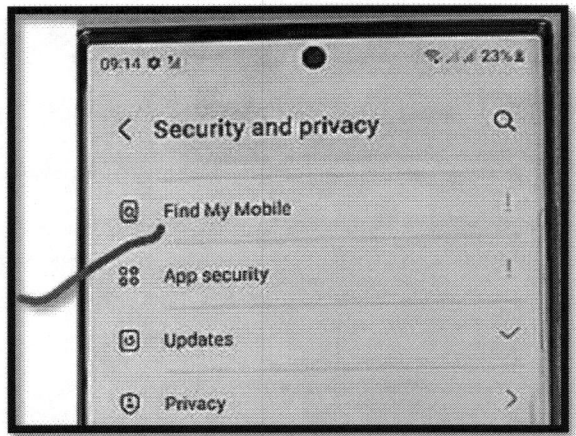

> **Allow this phone to be found** from the Settings menu.

- Press the **toggle switch to activate Find My Mobile** and access your Samsung account. Below are the choices available:
- **Allow this phone to be found**: Allow this feature to locate this device by turning it on.
- **Remote unlock:** To unlock and control your device from a distance, enable Samsung to store your password, pattern, or PIN.
- **Send last location**: When the amount of battery life is reduced, enable your device to send its last location to the Find My Mobile server.

Google Play Protect

Google Play Protect is a security service that guards Android devices against malware sometimes referred to as potentially harmful applications (PHAs). It is an inbuilt security feature on Android devices whose main job is to find and delete malicious software by continuously scanning installed apps on your device and apps downloaded from the Google Play Store.

- Select **Security and Privacy > App Security > Google Play Protect** from the Settings menu. Keep in mind that updates are automatically verified.

Security update

It's simple to find out when the security software was last updated and whether any newer versions are available.

- To view the most recent security update that is installed and find out if a newer version is available, navigate to **Settings > Security and Privacy > Updates > Security update.**

Permission manager

Applications may use device features (such as the camera, microphone, or location) even when you're not using them. This is especially true when the app is operating in the background. You have the option to have your device alert you when this occurs.

- Select **Security and Privacy > Privacy > Permission Manager from the Settings menu**.
- To choose which permissions you wish to receive notifications about, **tap a category, followed by an app.**

Note that a dialog box will appear the first time you use an app or service that requests access to specific features of your device and asks if you want to allow such access.

Samsung privacy

Samsung is a technology company that values user privacy. To that end, it has put in place several features and security measures. When experiencing technical issues, send Samsung diagnostic data about your device.

- To access Other privacy settings, navigate to **Security and Privacy > Privacy >**

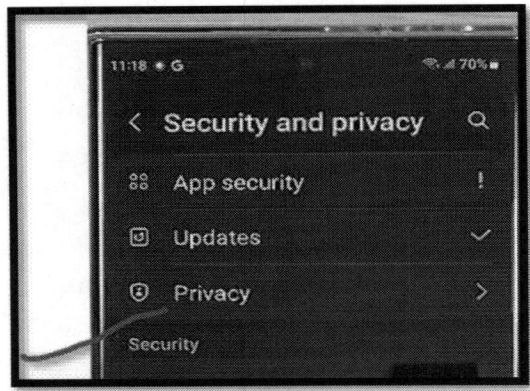

From Settings.

- To customize, select **Samsung and tap the corresponding options:**
  - **Samsung privacy**: Visit Samsung Privacy to view their privacy policies.
  - **Customization Service:** Permit Samsung to send you personalized recommendations and content.
  - **Send diagnostic data:** If you experience technical issues with your device, send diagnostic data about it to Samsung.

Google Privacy

Google has put in place several safeguards and features to protect user data across all of its products and services because it is dedicated to preserving user privacy. You can customize Google privacy and Android privacy features by using Google Privacy.

- Go to **Security and Privacy > Privacy > other privacy settings in Settings**.
- To modify privacy services, select them under Google.

Secure Folder

Your private apps and content, including contacts and images, are shielded from prying eyes with Secure Folder. Your files and applications remain safe even after the device has been unlocked. A distinct, secure storage space is called a Secure Folder. It is not possible to share data from Secure Folder to other devices using unapproved techniques like USB or Wi-Fi Direct. Any attempt to modify the software or alter the operating system will result in Secure Folder becoming automatically locked and unusable. Make sure to backup your data to a secure location before storing it in a secure folder.

Setting up Secure Folder

- Navigate to **Settings and press Privacy and Security > More security settings > Secure Folder.**
- To finish the setup, adhere to the instructions displayed on the screen. Tap **Turn on** when a pop-up window requesting that you reset the Secure Folder lock type using your Samsung account appears. You can reset the lock type with your Samsung account if you've forgotten it. You won't be able to reset the lock type if you don't activate this feature after you forget it. The Secure Folder screen and the Secure Folder app icon will be added to the Apps screen once the setup is finished. You have to use your preset lock method to unlock the Secure Folder app when it's locked. To modify the Secure Folder's name or icon, select **More options > Customize.**

Setting an auto lock condition for Secure Folder

- Select **More options > Settings > Auto lock Secure Folder** after launching the Secure Folder app.
- Choose a locking option. To manually lock your Secure Folder, select **Lock and exit from the More options menu.**

Moving content to Secure Folder

Transfer files, including images and videos, to the Secure Folder. Moving an image from the default storage to the Secure Folder can be done as follows.

- Select **More options > Add files when the Secure Folder app is open.**
- To move an image, select it, tap Images, and finally tap **Done.**
- Press **Move**. The chosen items will be transferred to the Secure Folder and removed from the original folder. Tap **Copy to copy an item.**

Moving content from the Secure Folder

Transfer files from the Secure Folder to the relevant app's default storage. An example of moving an image from the Secure Folder to the default storage is shown in the actions that follow.

- Select **Gallery when the Secure Folder app is open.**
- After choosing a picture, select **More > Move out of Secure Folder from the menu.** The chosen items will be transferred from the default storage to the Gallery.

Adding accounts

To get your accounts to sync with the apps in Secure Folder, add your Google, Samsung, and other accounts.

- Press **More options > Settings > Manage accounts > Add account** when the **Secure Folder app is open.**
- Choose a service for your account.
- To finish configuring your account, adhere to the on-screen directions.

Uninstalling Secure Folder

You can remove Secure Folder along with its contents and applications. Press **More Options> Settings > More settings > Uninstall when the Secure Folder app is open.**

- Tick Move media files out of **Secure Folder and tap Uninstall** to make a backup copy of the content before removing Secure Folder. Open the My Files app, and select **Internal storage > Download > Secure Folder** to view the data that has been backed up from Secure Folder.

Secure Wi-Fi

A service that protects your Wi-Fi network connection is called Secure Wi-Fi. To ensure that you can use Wi-Fi networks safely, it encrypts data while using them and disables tracking websites and apps. For instance, Secure Wi-Fi is automatically activated when utilizing an insecure Wi-Fi network in public areas like cafes or airports to prevent hackers from accessing your login credentials or tracking your online and app usage.

- To finish the setup, select **Security and Privacy > More security settings > Secure Wi-Fi** from the Settings screen, then follow the on-screen directions. You can view the history of how and when Secure Wi-Fi protected your network by selecting Protection activity.

The icon will show up in the status bar when Secure Wi-Fi is enabled.

- Wi-Fi network speed may decrease if this feature is used.
- The availability of this feature varies based on the Wi-Fi network, carrier, and model.

Selecting apps to protect using Secure Wi-Fi

Choose which apps to use Secure Wi-Fi to protect so that you can safely keep information safe from prying eyes, like your password or app usage history.

- Select **Security and Privacy > More security settings > Secure Wi-Fi > More options > Settings > Protected apps from the Settings screen. Then, tap the switches next to the apps that you wish to use Secure Wi-Fi to protect.**

Purchasing protection plan

Every month, you get a complimentary protection plan for Wi-Fi networks. Additionally, you can buy premium protection plans and benefit from temporary unlimited bandwidth protection.

- Toggle between **Security and Privacy > on the Settings screen. More security settings > Secure Wi-Fi.**
- Select **"Protection plan" Upgrade and choose your preferred plan.**
- Proceed with the instructions being displayed on the screen to complete the purchase.

Device Maintenance

The Samsung Galaxy S24 has a feature called Device Maintenance that assists users in managing and optimizing their device's performance. It has many tools and features to improve the device's security, battery life, and overall performance.

Quick optimization

By doing the following, the quick optimization feature enhances device performance:

- Locating and removing apps that consume an excessive amount of battery life.
- Removing pointless files and shutting down background-running apps.
- Looking for malicious software.

From Settings, select **Battery and Device Care> Optimize now** to activate the quick optimization feature.

Battery

See how the battery is used for the different things your device does.

- To access the following options, select **Settings > Battery and device care > Battery**:
- **Power saving**: Reduce background network usage, synchronization, and location checking to prolong battery life. When this mode is activated, you can select additional power-saving options to save even more energy.
- **Limits on background usage**: View apps you don't use frequently and set battery usage limits for them. Tap Put unused apps to sleep to turn this feature off.

- **Usage since last full charge**: See how much battery you've recently used by service, app, and time.
- **Wireless power sharing**: Enable wireless power-sharing by using the battery on your device to charge other compatible devices wirelessly.
- **Additional battery settings**: Set up additional notifications and battery settings.

Storage

View your storage space and usage in detail by file type and category.

- Select **Battery and Device Car e> Storage from the Settings menu.**
- For file management and viewing, tap a category.

Memory

Verify the available memory. To speed up your device, you can minimize the amount of memory you are using and close background apps.

- Select **Battery and Device Care > Memory from the Settings menu.** Both the used and free memory are displayed.
  - To maximize memory, tap **Clean now**.
  - To see the complete list of services and apps utilizing memory, tap **View more.**
  - Press the mark sign to add or remove these applications and services.
  - To see the apps and services that are part of this group, tap Apps not used recently. Press the mark sign to add or remove these applications and services.
  - To see a list of the apps that have been excluded, tap **Excluded apps.**
  - To select which apps to omit from memory usage assessments, tap **Add Apps.**
  - To choose how much internal storage to use as virtual memory to enhance app performance, tap **RAM Plus.**

Language and Input

Users of a Samsung Galaxy S24 can alter the language preferences for the device's keyboard input and user interface by going into the Language and Input settings. This section also offers options for configuring text-to-speech, keyboard settings, and other input-related features.

Change the device language

Languages can be added to your list and arranged based on your preferences. An app will switch to the next supported language in your list if it cannot run in your default language.

- Select **General Management > Language from the Settings menu**.
- Choose a language from the list by tapping **Add language.**
- To switch the device language, tap **Set as default.**
  - Select a different language from the list by tapping it, and then select **Apply.**

App languages

Select the default language for each app.

- Select **General Management > App languages from the Settings menu**.
- To modify the default language, tap **an app.**

Text-to-speech

Set up your TTS (text-to-speech) preferences. Voice Assistant is one of the accessibility features that uses text-to-speech (TTS).

- For options, select **General management > Text-to-speech from the Settings menu:**
  - **Preferred text-to-speech engine**: Select between Google and Samsung. To access options, tap Settings.
  - **Language**: Select the speech-language of choice.
  - **Speech rate**: Adjust the speech rate to speak the text at the desired pace.
  - **Pitch**: Determine the speech's pitch.
  - **Play**: Press to start a brief speech synthesis demonstration.
  - **Reset:** Adjust the pitch and speech rate.

Change the voice input language

Get language packs to utilize when not connected.

- Select **General Management > Voice input** from the Settings menu.
- Select a language pack to utilize voice input when not connected.

Keyboard list and default

You can adjust built-in keyboards, switch up your default keyboard, and adjust keyboard settings.

- Select **General Management > Keyboard list and set the following options as your defaults from Settings**:
- **Default keyboard**: Select a default keyboard for the menus and keyboards on your device.
- **Samsung keyboard**: Adjust the keyboard's settings.
- **Google Voice Typing:** Adjust Google Voice input settings.
- **Keyboard button on the navigation bar:** Activate the keyboard button located on the navigation bar to rapidly transition between keyboards.

Physical keyboards

If your device is linked to a physical keyboard, you can personalize the settings.

- Select **General Management from Settings**.
- Select an option after tapping **the Physical keyboard**:
    - **Display on-screen keyboard**: When using a physical keyboard, display the on-screen keyboard.
    - **Keyboard shortcuts:** Display on-screen instructions for each keyboard shortcut.
    - **Modify language shortcut**: On your physical keyboard, you can enable or disable language key shortcuts.

Mouse and trackpad

Set the button assignments and pointer speed for a mouse or trackpad that is optional.

- Select **General Management> Mouse and Trackpad from the Settings menu**.
    - **Pointer speed:** To move the pointer faster or slower, drag the slider to the right or left.
    - **Wheel scrolling speed**: Drag the slider to the right to scroll more quickly or to the left to scroll more slowly on a wheel.
    - Improve pointer accuracy by allowing the mouse cursor to move more or less quickly based on the speed at which the mouse is moved.
    - **Pointer size and color**: Modify the mouse pointer's size and color.
    - **Primary mouse button**: Select your primary mouse button from the Left or Right menu.
    - **Secondary button**: Select the mouse button's secondary function.
    - Select the function of your mouse's middle button.
    - **Additional Button 1**: Select an action for one more mouse button that is available.
    - **Additional Button 2**: Select an action for a second mouse button that is accessible.

Date and time

By default, the wireless network provides date and time information to your device. If you're not connected to the internet, you can manually adjust the time and date.

- Select **General Management > Date and time from the Settings menu**. There are the following choices available:
  - **Automatic date and time**: Date and time updates are automatically received from your wireless network. The following choices are accessible when you disable the automatic date and time:
    - **Set date**: Type in the day of the week.
    - **Set time**: Type in the time right now.
  - **Automatic time zone**: Make use of the time zone that your cellular network offers.
    - **Choose a time zone**: Pick a different time zone.
  - **Adapt your time zone to your location**: Get updates on time based on where you are.
  - **Employ the 24-hour format**: Decide on the display format for the time.

Customization service

Samsung apps, devices, and services are made to anticipate your needs and want and offer you personalized services astutely and cleverly. Based on data gathered about you and how you use Samsung's services, Samsung's Customization Service offers recommendations and tailored content to improve your user experience.

- Select **General Management > Customization service from the Settings menu.**

Accessibility

For those who require assistance with seeing, hearing, or using their device in other ways, there are accessibility settings. Accessibility services are extra features that facilitate everyone's use of the device.

Recommended for you

See a list of the accessibility features you are currently utilizing along with some suggested features you might want to turn on.

- To view recommendations, select **Accessibility > Recommended from the Settings menu.**

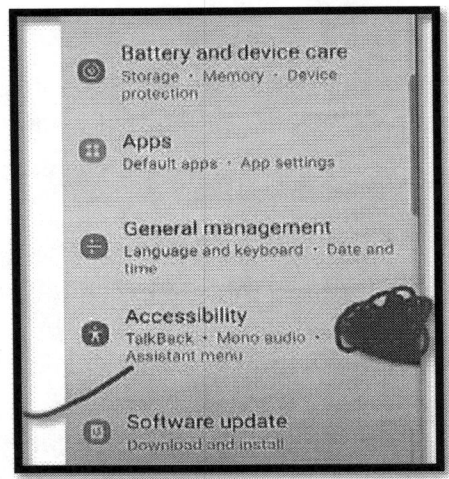

TalkBack

To navigate without seeing the screen, make use of specific controls and settings.

- Select **TalkBack**

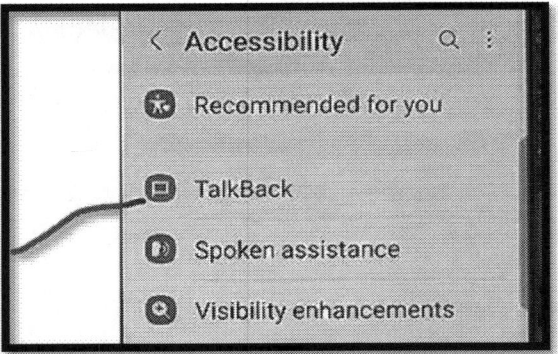

- **Under Accessibility in the Settings menu**.
- Toggle the feature on and select a customizable option by tapping:
- **TalkBack shortcut**: Select a shortcut to activate TalkBack instantly.
- **Settings**: Configure TalkBack's settings to help you more effectively.

Spoken assistance

To navigate without seeing the screen, make use of specific controls and settings.

- Select **Accessibility > Spoken assistance from the Settings menu.**

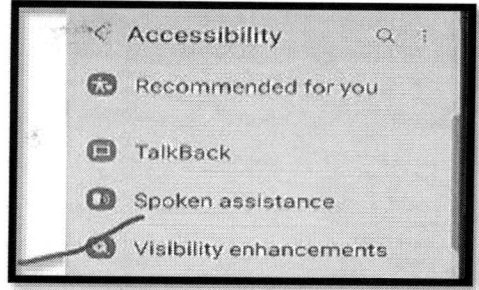

- **Toggle the feature on and select a customizable option by tapping it:**

  - **Talk aloud while entering text on the keyboard**: The gadget will read aloud whatever you type.

  - **Audio description**: When watching videos, automatically select the audio soundtrack that includes an audio description if it is available.

  - **Bixby Vision for accessibility**: Add modes to Bixby Vision for accessibility, such as reading aloud text, describing scenes, detecting colors, and more.

  - **Voice Label:** As you approach objects or locations, voice recordings can be written to NFC tags (not included) to provide you with information about them.

Colors and clarity

For easier viewing, you can change the texts and other screen elements' colors and contrast.

- Select **Accessibility > Visibility enhancements from the Settings menu**. Then, select an option:
- Select a display mode from the options, then hit **Apply**:
  - **Default**: The display mode by default.
  - **High contrast:** The following settings are activated; Reduce transparency and blur, remove animations, use dark mode, high contrast fonts, and high contrast keyboard.
  - **Big screen**: The font size, screen zoom, bold font, and highlight buttons have all been increased.
  - **High contrast theme**: To make viewing easier, adjust screen fonts and colors to create more contrast.
  - **High contrast fonts:** To make a font stand out more against the background, change its color and outline.

- **High contrast keyboard**: To improve the contrast between the keys and the background, resize and alter the color of the Samsung keyboard.
- **Button highlights:** To make buttons stand out more against the wallpaper, display buttons with tinted backgrounds.
- **Color inversion:** Change the text's color display from black on a white background to white text on a black background.
- **Color correction**: If certain colors are hard for you to see, change the screen's color.
- **Color filter:** If you're having trouble reading the text, change the colors on the screen.
- **Delete animations**: If you are motion-sensitive, get rid of some screen effects.
- **Minimize transparency and blur**: To improve readability, lessen the visual effects on menus and dialog boxes.
- **Extra dim:** To make viewing more comfortable, lower the screen's brightness beyond the minimum value. Press to see more choices.

Size and zoom

On your device, you can make shortcuts for accessibility features and enlarge supported screen elements.

- Select **Accessibility > Visibility enhancements from the Settings menu**. Then, select an option:
- **Magnification**: Use dramatic motions to increase the magnification, like double pinching, triple tapping, and dragging two fingers across the screen.
- **Magnifier:** Make use of the camera to enlarge your surroundings.
- **Pointer size and color**: If you have a connected mouse or touchpad, use a large pointer.
- **Font size and style:** Set the font style and size for the screen.
- **Screen zoom**: Set the degree of screen zoom.

Alternate input

Numerous inputs and controls are available for you to use to operate your device.

- Select **Accessibility > Interaction and Dexterity from the Settings menu**. Then, select an option:
- **Universal switch**: Use your personalized switches to operate your gadget.
- **Assistant menu:** Make devices more accessible to people with limited dexterity.
- **Voice Access:** Voice Access enables hands-free device control. To open apps, tap buttons, scroll, type, and more, use voice commands.

Interactions

The movements required answering calls and reacting to alerts and notifications can be made simpler.

Select **Accessibility > Interaction and Dexterity from the Settings menu**. Then, select an option:

Returning and taking calls:

- **Read caller names aloud**: When utilizing Bluetooth or headphones, hear the names of incoming calls read aloud.
- **Answer automatically**: If you're using Bluetooth or a headset, answer calls after a predetermined amount of time.
- **Turn up the volume to take calls**: To answer calls, press the Volume keys.
- **Press the Side key to end calls:** The Side key can be used to end calls.
- **Interaction control**: Customize the keyboard, hard keys, and screen interaction areas for enhanced control.

Touch Settings

Your screen can be adjusted to respond less strongly to touches and taps.

- Select **Accessibility > Interaction and Dexterity from the Settings menu**. Then, select an option:
  - **Touch and hold delay**: You can choose how long this action will take.
  - **Tap duration**: Define the minimum duration of an interaction for it to qualify as a tap.
  - **Ignore repeated touches**: Choose a window of time to disregard repeated touches.

Mouse and physical keyboard

Set up the physical keyboard and mouse that are connected.

- Select **Accessibility > Interaction and Dexterity from the Settings menu.** Then, select an option:
- **Auto action after pointer stops:** When the pointer stops over an item, take an automatic action by clicking on it.
- **Sticky keys:** You can enter keyboard shortcuts by pressing one key at a time by pressing a modifier key, such as Shift, Ctrl, or Alt, which stays pressed down when you press it.
- **Slow keys:** To prevent inadvertent key presses, specify the length of time a key must be held before it is detected as pressed.

- **Bounce keys**: Predict how long to wait before allowing a key to be pressed again to help prevent inadvertently pressing the same button more than once.

Digital-Wellbeing and Parental Control

The goals of the Digital Wellbeing and Parental Control features are to assist users in taking charge of their digital behavior, encourage a healthy balance between screen time and offline activities, and give parents the means to monitor and manage their kids' device usage. Modern smartphones and other digital devices frequently have these features built into the settings. To assist users in comprehending and controlling their smartphone usage, Digital Wellbeing is a collection of features and tools. With the information it offers about screen time, app usage, and notifications, users are better equipped to make decisions about their digital habits. To provide a secure and age-appropriate digital environment for their kids, parental control features are made to assist parents in monitoring and controlling their kids' device usage.

For the following features, select Digital Wellbeing and Parental Controls from the Settings menu:

- **To see the following, tap the Dashboard:**
  - **Screen time:** See each day's opening and usage of an app.
  - **Received notifications**: See the total number of notifications you receive from an app every day.
  - **Times opened/Unlocks**: View the number of times an app has been opened each day by selecting "Times opened/Unlocks."
  - Establish a goal for your screen time and check the average for each day.
  - **App timers**: Assign a daily duration to each app's use.
  - **Driving monitor:** Keep track of the apps you use most frequently and your screen time while linked to your car's Bluetooth system.
  - **Volume monitor**: Select a sound source to keep an eye on the volume and protect your ears.
  - **Parental controls**: Use Google's Family Link app to keep an eye on your kids' online activities. You can select apps, apply content filters, monitor screen time, and establish screen time limits.

Parental Control

By the use of the Google Family Link app, you can establish parental controls that will limit the apps that your child can access. After you have done so, you will be able to restrict their access to specific applications and monitor the amount of time they spend using their mobile device (phone or tablet).

Setting up parental control

- Navigate **to and also Open Settings then touch Digital Wellbeing and parental controls.**
- **Touch Parental controls then touch Get Started.**

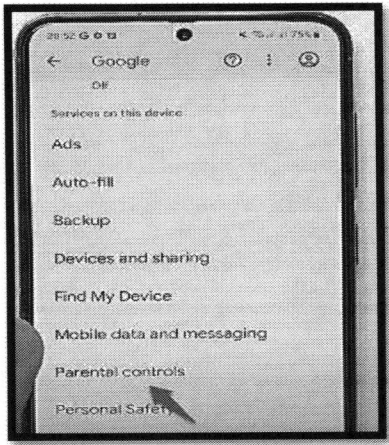

- Choose a **Child or teen based on the user.**

- Touch **Get Family Link and have Google Family Link installed.**
- Install the app only if it's required. Tap the **Open button** when the download is finished, read over the information, and then tap the **Get Started button.**
- If you have upwards of one Google account linked to the device you're using, select the one you want to use.
- The next step is to decide if the device will be utilized by the parent, the child, or the teen.

- Tap the **Next button** once you've established that the device you wish to monitor is within proximity. After reading the information, select **"I'm ready" from the menu**.
- Choose either **Yes or No**, based on whether or not your child already has a Google account.
- Tap the **Done button**, and then review the setup instructions for the device your child will use, and then touch **the OK button**.
- Download G**oogle Family Link for children and teens** onto the device that your child uses, and then enter the **Family Link setup code** that was provided to you.
- To successfully connect the two devices, you will need to follow the instructions that appear on the screens of both devices.
- After everything has been set up, you can use the **Family Link app** to keep a check on everything from a central location.

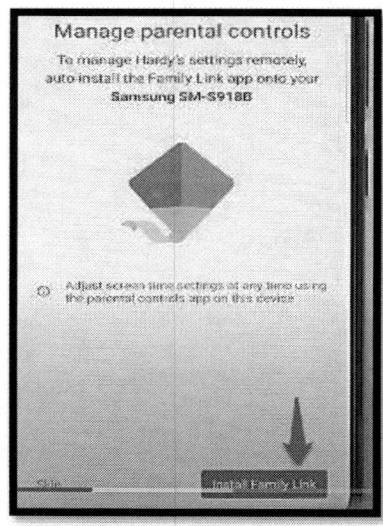

If there's ever a time when you need to keep an eye on more kids, all you have to do is launch the app and then touch the "Add" button (which looks like a plus sign) in the upper right corner of the screen. After reaching this point, you will need to follow the same steps again to join your child's Google account.

Terminate supervision of an account

It is important to remember that you will have to continue to monitor your child's profile until they are at least 13 years old. Google may continue to restrict access to its services for users of a certain age.

- Locate **the parent device then open the Google Family Link application**.

- Touch **the account of the child that you no longer want to supervise.**
- Touch **Manage beneath Settings then touch Account info**.

Samsung pass

Selecting a secure password manager is necessary to protect your passwords, but Samsung helps its users make the process easy. Many of the company's devices come with Samsung Pass, the password manager, preinstalled. Furthermore, Samsung Pass is a great way to keep your logins and passwords on your phone—even though it's most helpful for users who fully embrace Samsung's software ecosystem. Pass. It stores login credentials from apps and websites so you can access these services later on without having to enter your information. Your Samsung phone's Trust Zone, an isolated environment on the device that encrypts data to keep it safe, is where the service saves your login credentials. Samsung Pass can store notes, bank cards, and addresses in addition to usernames and passwords. These details can be added to any platform that is compatible with the Android autofill framework. Because Samsung Pass integrates with the Samsung keyboard, it offers an advantage over other password managers in that you can always access it, even on websites and applications without autofill. **Before making use of the Samsung pass take note of the following;**

- Only websites accessed through the Samsung Internet app can utilize the website sign-in feature. This feature might not be supported by all websites.
- Your device is the only place where registered biometric data is saved; it is not synchronized with servers or other devices.

Registering Samsung Pass

Make sure to register your biometric information with Samsung Pass before using it.

- Select **Security and Privacy> More security settings > Samsung Pass from the Settings screen**. To finish the setup, adhere to the instructions displayed on the screen.

Verify the Samsung account password

When you purchase content from the Galaxy Store, for instance, you don't need to enter your Samsung account password; instead, you can use your registered biometric data to verify your identity.

- Turn on the Verify with Samsung Pass feature by tapping the switch after selecting **More options > Settings > Account and syncing on the Samsung Pass main screen**.

Use Samsung Pass to sign in to websites

To log in to websites that support ID and password autofill, use Samsung Pass.

- Enter your ID and password on the website sign-in page, then click **the sign-in button**.
- Click **Sign in** with Samsung Pass and then tap Remember when a pop-up window asking to save the sign-in details appears.

Use Samsung Pass to sign in to apps

To log in to apps that support ID and password autofill, use Samsung Pass.

- After entering your ID and password on the app's sign-in page, tap **the sign-in button.**
- Tap **Save** when a pop-up window requesting that you save the sign-in details appears.

Signing in using passkeys

You can use a passkey stored in Samsung Pass to log in to apps and websites that support passkey-only logins rather than using your ID and password.

- Make a passkey on the app or website that you are currently using. Depending on the app or website, there may be differences in the process for making a passkey.
- Choose **Samsung Pass** when a pop-up window requesting that you save the passkey shows up.
- To store the passkey, adhere to the on-screen directions. Using the passkey that was saved in **Samsung Pass, you can now log in.**

Managing sign-in information

- Examine the list of websites and applications that you have configured to utilize Samsung Pass and adjust your login credentials.
- Choose an application or website from the list by tapping Apps/websites on the Samsung Pass home screen.
- To change your ID, password, and the name of the website or app, taps **Edit.** Tap **Delete** to remove your sign-in details.

Using Samsung Pass with websites and apps

You can sign in with Samsung Pass when using websites or apps that support it. On the Samsung Pass main screen, select **More options > Settings > Partners** to view the list of websites and apps that are compatible with Samsung Pass. Partners won't show up if there aren't any websites or apps that work with Samsung Pass.

- The websites and apps that are available might change based on the model or service provider.
- When using Samsung Pass to log in to websites or apps, Samsung is not liable for any loss or inconvenience.

Entering personal information automatically

When using apps that support autofill, you can use Samsung Pass to input personal data like your address or credit card information.

- Choose a **Private info option from the Samsung Pass main screen.**
- After entering the data, select **Save.** Now, you can use the biometric information you registered with Samsung Pass to have personal information automatically entered into compatible apps.

Deleting your Samsung Pass data

You can remove the biometric data, sign-in details, and app data associated with your Samsung Pass account.

- Select **More options > Settings > Devices using Samsung Pass > Leave Samsung Pass from the Samsung Pass home screen.**
  - The Samsung account you have will not expire.
  - On additional devices that are linked to your Samsung account, the Samsung Pass information will likewise be erased.

Activity

1. Setup faces recognition on your device.
2. Configure fingerprint recognition on your device.
3. Activate the Find My Mobile feature on your device.
4. Configure the various accessibility features on your device.
5. Set up parental control on your device.
6. Get your phone more secure with the use of Samsung Pass.

CHAPTER 11

YOUR APPS

This chapter brings to you the various applications that are available for you with the S24 series. You will learn about the Samsung apps, Google apps, and also Microsoft applications. You will also get to know about several other applications that can be of great use and how to effectively download them.

Galaxy Store

Get and install apps. Applications designed specifically for Samsung Galaxy devices can be downloaded.

- Launch **the Store application**. Use the tap to search for a keyword or browse apps by category.
- The carrier or model may determine whether this app is available.
- Select **Menu > Settings > Auto-update apps, choose an option, to adjust the auto-update settings.**

Play Store

Get and install apps. Launch the Play Store application. Apps can be found by keyword **search or by browsing by category.**

- To modify the auto-update configuration, press the icon of your account, choose **Settings > Network Preferences > Auto-update Applications, and then make a selection**.

Uninstalling or disabling apps

To choose an option, touch and hold an app.

- **Uninstall:** Remove downloaded applications.
- **Disable**: Turn off some of the built-in default apps that are locked to the device. This feature might not be supported by all apps.

Setting app permissions

Certain apps may require authorization to access or use data on your device to function properly. To view the permissions for your apps, go to **Settings and select Applications.** After choosing an app, select Permissions. You can modify and view the permissions of the application.

- Open Settings, select **Applications > More options > Permission manager** to view or modify the permission settings for individual apps. Choose a product and then an application.

Samsung Applications

During setup, the following apps might be downloaded over the air or come preloaded onto your device. Apps are available for download on the Google PlayTM store and the Galaxy Store.

Note however that service providers may offer different options.

- **AR Zone:** here you can access every feature related to Augmented Reality (AR) in a single location.
- **Bixby**: Personalized content is shown by Bixby depending on your interactions. Bixby makes recommendations for content you might enjoy based on your usage habits.
- **Galaxy Store**: Look for and download premium apps that are only compatible with Galaxy gadgets. It takes a Samsung account to download anything from the Galaxy Store.
- **Galaxy Wearable:** Use this app to pair your device with your Samsung Watch.
- Game Launcher: Organize all of your games in one location automatically. Please visit samsung.com/us/support/owners/app/game-launcher for additional information about Game Launcher.
  If the Apps list does not display Game Launcher, select **Advanced Features> Game Launcher** from the Settings menu.
- **Penup**: Browse the pages for something to add to your collection, post pictures, or leave comments on other people's creations (Galaxy S24 Ultra only). This group unites all who paint, sketch, scribble or draw with the S Pen.
- Samsung Free: Get free access to live TV shows, articles, and news from a variety of sources, and interactive games.
- **Samsung Global Goals**: With the help of this app's advertisements, you can find out more about the Global Goals initiative and donate to support these causes.
- **Samsung Members**: With your Galaxy device, do more and get more. Take advantage of DIY support resources and member-only experiences and content. Your device might come with Samsung Members preinstalled, or you can download and install it from the Google Play or Galaxy stores.
- **Samsung TV Plus**: Take advantage of free entertainment, news, and more on your mobile devices and Samsung TV.

- **Samsung Wallet**: You can use your device to make payments with Samsung Wallet. Almost everywhere you can swipe or tap your credit card, it will be accepted. It's necessary to have a Samsung account.
- **Smart Switch:** Transfer contacts, pictures, and other files from your old device to Smart Switch.
- **Smart Things**: With SmartThings, you can customize your home environment to meet your unique needs by controlling, automating, and monitoring it from a mobile device. The app allows you to connect one device at a time or multiple devices simultaneously. Examine your devices' status by glancing at the dashboard.

Note that the Samsung warranty does not cover errors or defects in non-Samsung connected devices; for assistance, get in touch with the non-Samsung device manufacturer.

Google Apps

Google offers business, social media, and entertainment apps. Certain apps might require a Google Account to use them. **Check out the help menu of each app to learn more about it.**

- **Chrome**: Use it to explore websites and do information searches.
- **Gmail**: Use the Google Mail service to send and receive emails.
- **Maps**: Access location, look up your location on a map, and search the globe details for a variety of nearby locations.
- **YT Musi**c: Take advantage of the diverse music and videos offered by YouTube Music. You can also listen to and access the music libraries that are saved on your device.
- **Google TV**: Get or rent videos from the Play Store, including TV shows and movies.
- **Drive**: Save your files to the cloud, view them from any location, and share them with
  others.
- **YouTub**e: Share your own or other people's videos with the world.
- **Photos**: Find, organize, and edit every photo and video you have from different sources in one location.
- **Google**: Look up products on the web or on your mobile device.
- **Meet**: Organize, start, or participate in video conferences.
- **Messages**: Use your computer or device to send and receive messages and to share different types of content, including photos and videos.
- **Assistant**: Make use of the features on your device or do a voice search for information.

Microsoft Applications

Your device might come with the following Microsoft apps preloaded. Apps are available for download on the Google Play store and the Galaxy Store.

- **Outlook**: Outlook allows you to access email, calendar, contacts, tasks, and more.
- **Microsoft 365**: With the Microsoft 365 app, enjoy Word, Excel, and PowerPoint on your mobile device.
- **OneDrive**: You can use your free online OneDrive® account to store and share documents, videos, images, and more. You can access your account from a computer, tablet, or phone.

Samsung Members

Samsung Members allows users to ask questions and report errors, in addition to providing support services like diagnosing device issues. Additionally, you can check the most recent news and advice or exchange information with other members of the Galaxy users' community. You can get assistance from Samsung Members to fix any issues you may run into with your device.

Samsung Kids

To make sure kids use the device in a fun and safe way, you can set usage limits, prevent kids from using specific apps, and customize settings. Swipe down to reveal the notification panel, and then tap (Kids). If the quick settings panel does not contain (Kids), drag the button over to add it by tapping the **pen icon > Edit.** Upon initiating Samsung Kids for the first time or following a data reset, adhere to the on-screen guidance to finalize the configuration. Choose the desired app from the Samsung Kids screen.

Closing Samsung Kids

- Press **the Back button or choose More options > Close Samsung Kids** to end Samsung Kids. Then, enter your unlock code.

Samsung Global Goals

The United Nations General Assembly established the Global Goals in 2015, some of which are geared toward building a sustainable society. These objectives can halt climate change, combat inequality, and eradicate poverty.

Discover more about the global goals and get involved in the movement for a better future with Samsung Global Goals.

Samsung Shop / Find

Even if your device is not linked to a network, you can still find it. Additionally, you have the option to present to other people to see where you are. Launch the Find application. Furthermore, Samsung offers a mobile shopping service called Samsung Shop. Obtain deals or information about the goods and services offered by Samsung and its partners. Launch the Samsung Shop application.

Galaxy Wearable

You can control your wearables with the help of the Galaxy Wearable app. You can personalize the wearable device's settings and apps by connecting it to your phone.

Launch the Wearable application. Press Keep your phone connected to the wearable gadget. Comply with the on-screen guidelines to complete the setup. For further details on connecting and utilizing the wearable with your device, consult the user manual that comes with it.

How to Download New Apps

Best Free Apps to Download for the New Samsung Galaxy S24

Sketchbook

The S-Pen is one of the Samsung Galaxy S24 Ultra's more distinctive features. Moreover, there's no better way to utilize this stylus than by making sketches on your gadget. The majority of digital artists use the Sketchbook app because of its wide selection of tools, clear interface, and minimalistic design. The brushes can be altered to produce the ideal strokes that precisely replicate the original. Additionally, the app has stroke tools, rulers, and guides to help you draw with accuracy. Although it is free to download, there's a chance that some features are protected by a paywall.

INKredible

INKredible is the only app you need if you're looking for one for taking notes and doodling. This app virtually perfectly captures the experience of writing on paper. I appreciate the app's simple user interface and focus-free notepad. The screen is free of toolbars and banner advertisements. Its notepad's grid paper design is also very attractive. The application detects even the smallest strokes with minimal latency. The software only accepts input from the S-Pen thanks to Automatic Palm Rejection.

DocuSign

The ability to scribble your e-signature without using your finger is one of the best things about owning a stylus. You can use the S-Pen on your S24 Ultra to sign any document using DocuSign. With this app, users can quickly scribble their signature wherever needed in any document by opening it in any of the major file formats. This app allows you to scan a paper document and turn it into a digital file. Use Docusign to store your signature, then quickly copy and paste it to the appropriate place on any document.

Adobe Acrobat

Our favorite app for general document management is Adobe Acrobat. You can read and edit documents in a variety of formats with ease if you have the Acrobat Reader. Using this app to sign and annotate documents is as simple as sharing them with friends, family, and coworkers. Additionally, it includes a useful PDF converter that enables you to convert Word, Excel, picture, and other document files into PDF files. If you are in front of a paper document, you can use Adobe Acrobat to scan it, sign it, and create a PDF file.

Adobe Premiere Rush

Making videos is a great way to gauge a smartphone's power. Graphically demanding games might be supported by your device, but editing videos for extended periods strains the processor and quickly depletes the battery. One of the few smartphones that can do this task flawlessly is the Samsung Galaxy S24 Ultra. And Adobe Premiere Rush is the ideal app to use for this task. The vast array of tools in this app is easily accessible to the typical user. You won't have any problems using this app, even if you're not very good at editing videos.

KineMaster

You might already be familiar with KineMaster if you create content online. For editing your Reels, TikToks, Shorts, and even long-form videos, this app is ideal. Tons of royalty-free sound effects, templates, music, and other items are available in its Asset Store to help you spice up your videos. With KineMaster, you can easily cut, trim, merge, split, and splice your videos while adding the appropriate effects. It ranks among the best video editing apps thanks to features like keyframe animation, chroma key, stop motion editing, and background removal.

Microsoft SwiftKey AI Keyboard

Microsoft updated the SwiftKey keyboard app with AI features quite quickly. Using the keyboard itself, you can use the Bing chatbot to compose a text message or email. Depending on the circumstance, you can use the chatbot to change the tone to casual, friendly, polite, professional, or social before clicking send. The possibilities are endless when you can use the phone's keyboard to interact with a chatbot. Not sure what to say in the caption of an Instagram Story? Submit the task to the chatbot. Reach a standstill during a discussion? Additionally, Bing AI can assist you with that. Microsoft SwiftKey is among the greatest keyboard applications available for your new Samsung Galaxy S24 Ultra, in our opinion.

Music Time Travel

The app "Rewind: Music Time Travel" is what you need if you want to discover new music. With this app, you can travel through time and discover all of your favorite genres from previous decades. Rewind is a musical journey that spans from the psychedelic rock of the 1960s to the grunge and shoegaze of the 1990s. You can look through all of the hits from a specific year by navigating to that one. The app provides quick links to YouTube, Spotify, Tidal, Apple Music, and other music services, as well as 30-second song previews.

ChatGPT

AI has completely changed and become more widely available thanks to Open AI's ChatGPT. Although it took some time for its Android app to appear in the Google Play Store, once it does, it's impossible to put down. ChatGPT can do everything, including poetry and coding. It can assist you in generating original ideas and implementing them. The AI chatbot's conversational style, which lets you adjust the outcomes and provide feedback, is its best feature. To acquire knowledge on a novel topic, just request the chatbot to elucidate it in an easily understood language. It is even possible to request that it cite its sources and suggest related reading.

Character AI

Have you ever wished you could converse with a fictional character in fiction? Fortunately, you no longer need to imagine it. Character AI enables you to select a character and engage with it in any way you choose by utilizing the strength of extensive language models. You can choose from hundreds of user-generated personas or try out a fictional character from a video game or film. These personas aren't limited to fictional characters either—you can also communicate with bots that are modeled after well-known people and celebrities.

Best Free Apps to Download for the New Samsung Galaxy S24

Below is a combination of applications you almost cannot do without. Read up carefully and learn more about these amazing applications.

Travel booking applications - Airbob and Booking.com

Booking.com is a convenient travel service that enables users to book a room in any of more than 470,000 hotels, hostels, motels, flats, and other types of accommodations located all over the world. Booking.com, which is present in more than 200 countries around the world, provides all of the in-depth information that you require before going anywhere. You can find out which rooms are available in any location you want to visit by using the official Booking app. This app displays room pricing and availability, in addition to real images and reviews written by other Booking customers. Booking.com has more than eight million photographs of different hotel rooms and more than thirty million reviews written by guests that are honest and objective. You will be able to make an informed decision about where you will stay if you have access to all of this information as well as that which is supplied directly by the hotels and hostels. It should come as no surprise that the search tool on Booking.com enables users to apply a wide variety of search filters, which can be as specific as the location within the city, the price, the kind of housing, and so on. Booking.com is an app that absolutely everyone who wants to go on vacation and needs to choose a great hotel that satisfies all of their preferences should have on their phone. In 2022, the mobile application for Booking.com was the online travel agency app that received the most downloads all around the world. During that specific year, this app had a total of approximately 80 million downloads across both iOS and Google Play. The Airbnb app came in at number two on the list, having been downloaded over 52 million times.

Caller ID App- Truecaller

TrueCaller is a technology that gives you the ability to identify every incoming call, allowing you to learn the identity of the person trying to get in touch with you even before you pick up the phone. This implies that you can prevent any unwanted numbers from ever calling you again by blocking their phone numbers. In addition to the caller identification feature, which can only be utilized if you are connected to the internet via a Wi-Fi or 3G network, TrueCaller comes with many other useful functions. For instance, you can customize the screen that appears when your friends and contacts call by uploading photographs from social networking sites like Facebook, Twitter, or Google +.

TrueCaller will inform you, if you get a call from an unknown number, of the total number of other users who have reported the number as being unwelcome. This allows you to determine in a short amount of time whether or not the call is entertaining or crucial. TrueCaller is helpful software for anyone who has had it to the breaking point with telemarketers and other types of unwanted calls. After you have this software installed, you will never again have to deal with calls that are not wanted.

Photo Editing Software- Picsart

Considered to be one of the most potent design studios that can be carried around in the palm of your hand. PicsMaster Photo Editor is the best all-in-one editor available, and it can satisfy all of your requirements for altering photographs. This is the method to accomplish it if you're seeking a simple technique to make photographs that have a one-of-a-kind appearance and convey a message at the same time! Photos of any kind, including selfies, culinary, architectural, scenery, and fashion, can be edited quickly and easily. Make use of things within the application that you have created, such as memes, masks, fonts, captions, quotes, and watermarks. You may add gorgeous filters and photo effects, stunning artwork and typography, an ever-growing variety of patterns, light FX, textures, borders, designs, and more to your photographs, and then share them on the social networks of your choice. To generate results that give the impression that they were created by a professional photographer or graphic artist, all you need is a Picture Editor. This is the program's greatest strength. This application was developed to be user-friendly and speedy so that everyone may take advantage of its features.

Video editing software: InShot

The photo and video editing tool known as InShot Editor was developed specifically to enhance the final product of any video that you intend to post to your Instagram account. It also enables you to enhance photographs and, as expected, save modified films to the storage space available on your smartphone. In the section devoted to video editing, you will discover a lot of fascinating tools. For instance, if a video was shot in the vertical format, you have the option to either enlarge or center the image, or you can create a nice blur effect that is placed behind the image. You also have the option to apply filters, insert text, add music, and even add emojis to your video. After you have finished, all that is left to do is select the quality of the video that you wish to save. You will also find a wide variety of editing choices for your images. You can trim the image, apply any one of more than a dozen distinct filters, adjust the brightness and saturation, add any one of hundreds of stickers, and a great deal more. In a nutshell, you can give any image a completely different appearance. Although its primary purpose is to facilitate the production of material for Instagram, the InShot Editor is a robust picture and video editor that enables you to make adjustments to videos and still images before saving them directly to the memory of your smartphone.

Video chat app - Google Meet

The Google Duo app is a mobile program that enables users to communicate with one another using video chat. In addition to this, using it is a breeze, and the comfort level is through the roof. Nevertheless, to make use of it, you will first need to connect the app to a working phone number. In that case, you won't be able to participate in any video chats with other people. The user interface of Google Meet is extremely straightforward despite its uncluttered appearance.

You'll be able to view the image that your device's camera is taking on the screen of your device, and this will be the case for both your front and back cameras. This is accomplished by pressing a single button, which gives you access to hundreds of your contacts. And that wraps things up! If someone contacts you using Google Meet, you'll be able to view their image as soon as the call comes in, but the other person won't be able to see you until you pick up the phone and answer it. This way, you'll always be aware of exactly who is calling you, and you'll even be able to identify them before beginning a video call. Google Meet is the company's endeavor to deliver a video calling service that is user-friendly, lightning-quick, and safe. And this is just what the users of Google Meet are provided with.

Scan menu barcodes - Google Lens

Google Lens is an app that lets you utilize the camera on your device to learn more about your surroundings and uncover new information. The US technology giant also boasts a large database, which allows the tool to recognize virtually everything. One of the functions that Google Lens is capable of performing is identifying any object of clothing or piece of furniture that interests you while you are out and about. Simply concentrate on the item in question and the instrument will reveal information regarding the product. When you need to locate a store that carries a particular item, you will discover that this information is really helpful.

In addition, Google Lens can identify flora and animals. You will be able to learn about each living creature you come across anywhere in the globe, as well as identify new species of animals and plants that you haven't seen before thanks to this method. If you have an Android device, you may use Google Lens to determine the species of any animal or plant you come across. All of them come with the quality assurance stamp offered by Google. Unquestionably, a device that can assist you in gaining a deeper comprehension of the world around you and, in the interim, help you extricate yourself from more than one sticky situation.

Document scanning software - Adobe Scan

With the camera on your Android device and the Adobe Scan software, you can quickly and easily scan any document. With it, you will be able to turn any hard copy into a PDF file, which you can then either store in the memory of your device or send using any app. The scanning feature in Adobe Scan is user-friendly and produces reliable results. The only thing you need to do is lock the camera's focus on the page you want to scan, give the document a second to be scanned, and then work as hard as you can to hold the camera motionless. The application will detect the document and then do a scan of it without requiring the user to manually press any buttons. When you scan a page, the information will be saved as a PDF file that can later be accessed. After you have finished scanning, the only thing left to do is complete your PDF and make sure that everything is exactly how you want it to be. You are free to rearrange the pages in any way you see fit, and doing so will help you check that none of them were overlooked by accident. You are also able to make adjustments to the colors on any of the pages, or you can even change the entire document to black and white. Adobe Scan is a great document-scanning application that is on par with the remarkable CamScanner in terms of features and functionality. When you save documents using Adobe Scan, those documents will also be stored in your own Adobe account.

Health and Fitness - Samsung Health

The Samsung Health app is a fitness tracker that monitors your workouts, as well as your calorie consumption and sleep patterns. It is the workout app that comes preinstalled on Galaxy watches, and it comes with a broad variety of functions that can assist you in better managing your health and visualizing your progression. You can determine your fitness objectives, compete against your friends, and even take part in worldwide fitness competitions. You may also view handpicked videos that were created by people who are specialists in the field of fitness if you feel like you need some assistance getting into shape. The videos cover a wide range of topics relevant to fitness and health, including weight loss, growing muscle, fitness for women, endurance training, mindfulness, and jogging, amongst others. The user interface of the application is both attractive and straightforward, making it suitable for novices as well as experienced users. A weekly review of your activities, nutrition, and sleep, among other things, is available to view. You will be awarded a badge to serve as a visual representation of your fitness journey's progression each time you reach a new level of accomplishment.

App Locker - App Lock

AppLock is a simple program that gives you the ability to lock practically any kind of file that is stored on your Android device. You can lock not just your applications, which prevents anyone from accessing them or uninstalling them, but also your images, videos, contacts, and individual messages. The application has a straightforward method of operation. To begin, you will need to generate a numeric password to access the application that you intend to safeguard. After that point forward, whenever you open that particular app, it will request that you enter the password that you have previously established. This password window will not permit it to be removed from the system by any other user, even if they try. The nice part about this software is that you may hide its icon so that nobody knows that you have it installed on your smartphone. But, they will discover that you have it installed on your device if it asks them to enter the relevant password at some point.

Activity

1. Make a list of Samsung, Google, and Microsoft applications.
2. Download new applications on your phone.
3. Mention the 5 best free applications you can download.

CHAPTER 12

USING THE CAMERA

You can take pictures in various shooting modes and also record videos under this section. To get the best of the use of the Samsung Galaxy S24, take a look at certain camera etiquettes below.

Camera etiquette

- It is forbidden to take images or videos of other individuals without their consent.
- If taking photos or recording videos is against the law, do not do so.
- Avoid taking photos or videos in areas where you might infringe upon the privacy of others.

Using the camera button

- To capture a video, simply press **and hold the camera button.**

- You can record a video without holding down the camera button by **dragging it to the icon.**

- Swipe the camera button to the edge of the display and hold it to capture burst shots. You can make GIFs by tapping on the preview screen and then tapping the **Swipe Shutter button to create a GIF.**
- You can move the camera button anywhere on the screen and take more convenient photos if you add another one. To activate the **Floating Shutter button switch**, select **Settings > Shooting methods** from the preview screen and tap it.

Setting the Shooting mode

Drag the modes to the desired location after selecting **MORE** from the list, then tap the **Add icon to edit the shooting modes list.**

Using zoom features

- By employing the rear camera, choose **your preferred zoom icon on the preview screen to zoom in or out.**

- When you tap the zoom icon, a list of zoom levels appears from which you can **choose your preferred zoom level.**
- You can pinch, spread two fingers apart, or drag **the zoom icon on the preview screen to fine-tune the zoom.**
- A zoom guide map that shows where you are zooming in on the image will appear if the zoom ratio goes above a certain threshold.

Locking the focus (AF) and exposure (AE)

If the subject or light source changes, you can lock the focus or exposure on a specific area to stop the camera from making automatic adjustments. To focus, touch, **and hold the region;** the focus and exposure settings will be locked once the AF/AE frame appears on the region. After taking a photo, the setting stays locked.

The availability of this feature varies based on the shooting mode.

Photo mode

Depending on the environment, the camera automatically modifies the shooting settings. To take a picture, select **PHOTO** from the shooting modes list and press **the shutter.**

Changing the resolution

High-resolution photos are possible. To take a picture and adjust the resolution to your preference, tap 12M in the shooting options menu. The model may have an impact on the resolution.

Shot suggestions

By identifying the subject's position and angle, the camera makes recommendations for the best composition for the image. To activate the Shot suggestions switch, repeatedly tap the screen in preview mode.

- Select **PHOTO** from the list of shooting modes. There will be a preview screen with a guide.

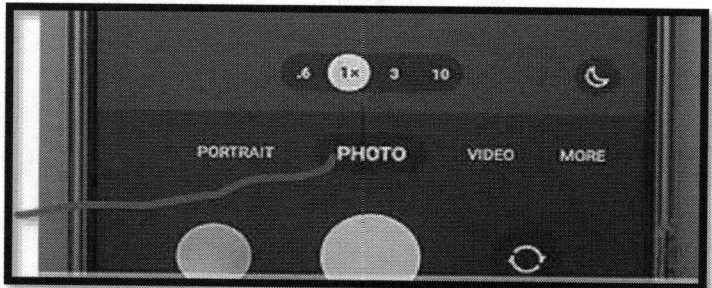

- Aim the guide directly at the subject. When the composition is recognized by the camera, the suggested composition shows up on the preview screen.
- Slide **the device to align the guide with the suggested composition**. The guide will turn yellow when the perfect composition is reached.
- To snap a photo, tap **the shutter.**

Taking selfies

You can use the front camera to snap pictures of yourself.

- Swipe left or right on the preview screen, or tap to **switch to the front camera for selfies.**

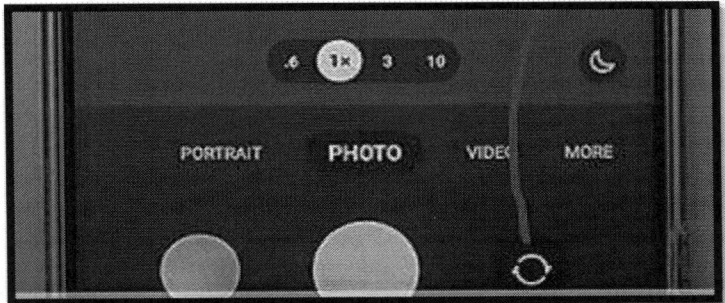

- Turn to face the front camera lens. Tap to take wide-angle photos of people or the scenery while taking a self-portrait.
- To take a picture, tap t**he shutter.**

Take clear close-up pictures (Galaxy S24 Ultra)

Capture crisp, up-close images of your subject.

- Press **1x** on the preview screen.
- Approach the subject with the camera close.
- Press the **shutter icon** when a yellow camera appears to snap a photo.

Applying filters and beauty effects

Before snapping a photo, you can choose a filter effect and alter facial features like your skin tone or face shape.

- Select the **Effects icon** from the preview screen.
- Choose **your effects and snap a photo**. You can download filters by tapping the **Add icon**, or you can make your filter by selecting an image from the Gallery with a desired color tone.

Taking Pictures

- Launch the Camera application. Alternatively, you can drag to the left on the locked screen or press the Side button twice to launch the application.

Note the following

- When you launch the Camera app from a locked screen or when the screen is off and the screen lock method is enabled, certain camera features are not accessible.
- When not in use, the camera turns off automatically.
- Certain techniques might not be accessible based on the model or carrier.
- Wherever the camera is supposed to focus, tap the image on the preview screen. Drag the adjustment bar that appears above or below the circular frame to change the brightness of images.
- To take a photo, tap **the shutter icon**. You can swipe left or right on the preview screen or drag the shooting modes list to the left or right to change the shooting mode.

To get the best shots when making use of your camera ensure you consider the following points; Depending on the camera being used and the shooting mode, different preview screens may appear.

- If the topic is close, the focus might not be obvious. Capture images or videos at a reasonable distance.
- Try cleaning the camera lens and taking another shot if your photos come out grainy.
- Verify that there are no contaminants or damages on the lens. If not, the gadget might not function correctly in certain modes that call for high resolutions.
- The camera on your device has a wide-angle lens. Light distortion is normal in wide-angle photos and videos and does not signal a problem with the device's performance.
- Depending on the resolution, a video's maximum capacity may change.
- The disparity in temperature between the exterior and interior of the camera cover can cause the device to fog up or produce condensation when it is subjected to abrupt fluctuations in air temperature. When using the camera, try to stay away from such situations. If fogging does happen, let the camera air dry at room temperature before snapping photos or shooting videos to avoid grainy images.

Different ways to save photos and videos

This section discusses the various ways in which you can have your photos and videos saved;

Create an album

You can create an album by either the year, the event, or anything you deem fit.

When albums are created it helps you sort images and videos accordingly such that when you need to locate an image or video much later, it will be done with so much ease. Follow the steps below to create albums;

- Open the **Gallery app and touch Albums > Album** to have an album created.

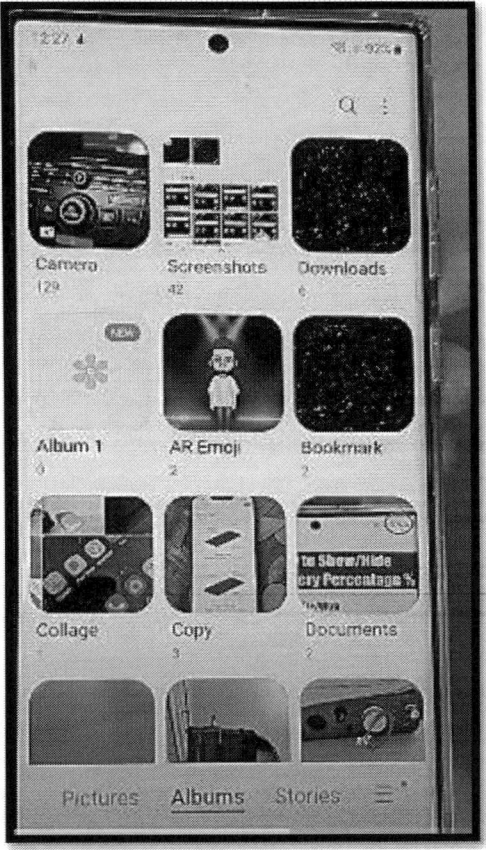

- Choose **the images or videos** you would like to copy or move them to a specific album that you have created.

The device will read the time and place stamps on the photos and videos you take or save, organize them, and then generate stories based on the content.

- Select **a story by launching the Gallery app** and tapping the Stories tab. The options available, when you click the menu button (three dots), include editing the story's content and renaming it. By selecting **the menu button (three dots)** and then selecting **Create story** from the stories list, you can manually generate new stories.

Save or sync your photos and videos on OneDrive

Ensuring that files are well saved and protected is very paramount to almost everyone. No one wants to wake up to deal with lost documents hence the need to have your files saved in a cloud setting such as OneDrive.

To finish the sync,

- Launch the **Gallery app, touch the cloud icon**, and then complete the on-screen prompts. Photos from the Gallery app will be uploaded to the cloud and vice versa.

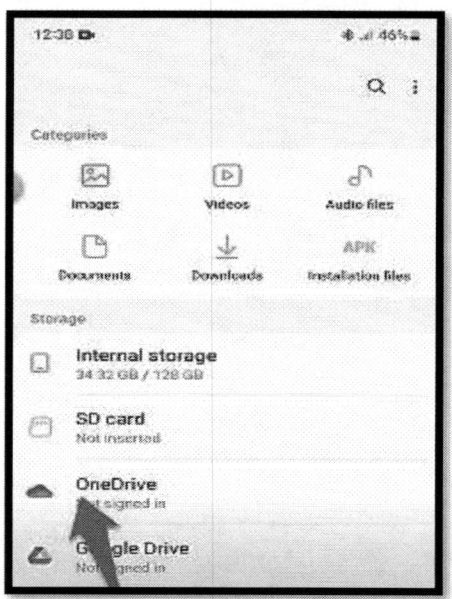

Your captured images and videos will be automatically uploaded to the cloud when the Gallery app is synced with cloud storage. Any of your cloud-stored photos and videos can be seen in the Gallery app, regardless of the device you're using to view them. Note that when you attach your Samsung account and Microsoft account together, you will be able to configure the cloud storage as Microsoft OneDrive.

Video mode

Depending on the environment, the camera automatically modifies the shooting settings.

- **To record a video, select VIDEO from the list of shooting modes.**
  - Press the camera switch icon or swipe the preview screen to alternate between the front and rear cameras while recording.
  - Press to take a picture of the video as it's being recorded.

- Point the camera in that direction and use the zoom to record the sound from that direction at a higher volume while you're filming a video.
- **To end the video recording, tap the stop icon.**
  - To keep your device from overheating, the video quality may decrease if you use the video zoom feature for an extended time while recording.
  - Low light conditions may prevent the optical zoom from functioning.

Changing the resolution

Up to 8K resolution can be achieved when recording high-definition videos. To adjust the resolution to your preferred setting and capture a video, simply tap the shooting options menu. Play the video in the Gallery app after you've completed recording it. A frame that you like can be tapped to save it as an image.

Stabilizing videos (Supersteady)

To further stabilize videos when there is a lot of shaking during recording, use the Super steady feature.

- Select **VIDEO** from the list of shooting modes, then tap **the shooting options** to activate it before starting to record a video.

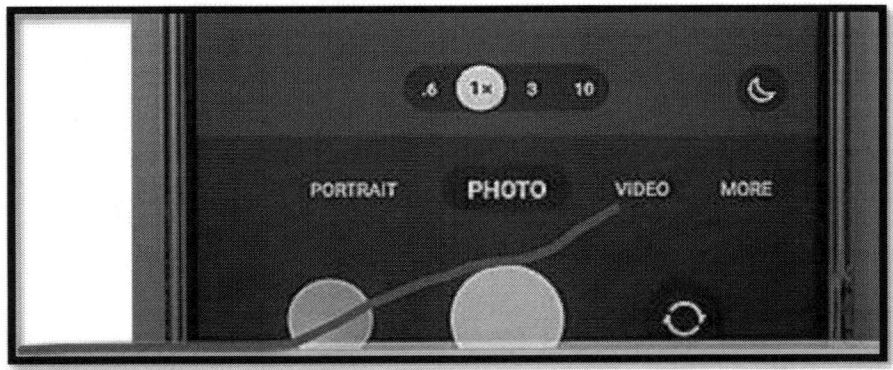

Using the auto-framing feature (Changing the shooting angle and zoom by tracking people)

When capturing videos, you can program the device to automatically adjust the zoom and shooting angle by identifying and following people.

- Select **VIDEO** from the list of shooting modes, tap to activate it, and then record a video.
- Tap the **frame that appears** around the person to track them, change the shooting angle, and zoom in on them. Press the frame once more to disable tracking.

Dual rec mode

Use two cameras at once to record videos. Each camera's video can be edited and saved independently.

Additionally, you have the option of playing the videos in split view or picture-in-picture mode.

- Select **MORE > DUAL REC** from the list of shooting modes.
- Press, choose two lenses, and press **OK.**
    - Press to save the videos from each camera individually.
    - Tap to switch the screen.
- To capture a video, tap **the recording button.**
- To end the video recording, tap **the stop button.**

Controlling the picture-in-picture window while playing the video

When recording or playing a video, you can adjust the picture-in-picture window's size and position if you have the screen in a picture-in-picture view.

- To save videos as separate files, tap the preview screen's saving option.
- To capture a video, tap the record icon. Before and during recording, you can adjust the picture-in-picture window's size and position.
    - Press **and hold the picture-in-picture window to make it larger.**
    - Drag the **picture-in-picture window to any desired location.**
- To end the video recording, tap **the stop button**. While the video is playing, you can also manipulate the picture-in-picture window. Launch the Gallery app, pick the video, and then select **More options > Open in Video Player**, or you can tap the preview thumbnail on the preview screen.

Single-take mode

Capture multiple images and videos in one shot. Your device chooses the best picture automatically and produces videos with repeated scenes or pictures with filters.

- Select **MORE > SINGLE TAKE** from the list of shooting modes.

- To record the desired scene, tap **the shutter icon.**
- Either launch the Gallery app and choose the file, or tap the preview thumbnail on the preview screen.

Portrait mode / Portrait video mode

You can take images or videos where the subject is well-defined and the background is blurred by using the Portrait or Portrait video modes. After snapping a photo, you can also edit and add a background effect.

- Select **PORTRAIT or MORE > PORTRAIT VIDEO** from the list of shooting modes.

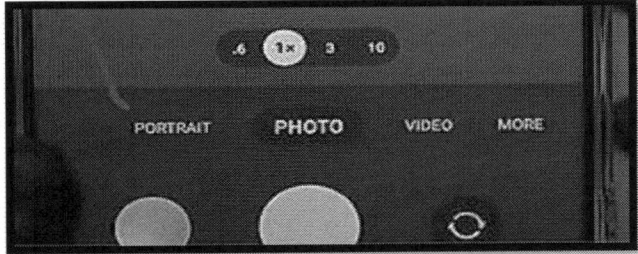

- Choose your preferred background effect by **tapping the background icon**. Drag the adjustment bar to change the background effect's intensity.

- Press **the shutter button** to take a picture or the record icon to record a video when **Ready** shows on the preview screen.

Take note of the following;

- The shooting mode may affect the available options.
- Make use of this feature in a well-lit area.
- **In the following circumstances, the background blur might not be applied correctly:**
  - Either the object or the person is moving.
  - The topic is transparent or thin.
  - The background and the subject are both of the same color.
  - The background or subject is simple.

Pro mode / pro video mode

Take images or record videos while manually modifying the ISO and exposure values, among other shooting parameters.

- Select **PRO or PRO VIDEO** from the list of shooting modes. After making adjustments to the settings and selecting options, tap **the shutter button to snap a photo or the record icon to record a video.**

Below are the other available shooting options;

- **ISO**: Decide on an ISO number. It manages the light sensitivity of the camera. For stationary or well-lit objects, use low values. Higher values apply to objects that move quickly or have poor lighting. Higher ISO settings, however, may cause noise in images or videos.
- **SPEED**: Modify the shutter speed. A slower shutter speed lets in more light, which brightens the image or video. This works perfectly for images or videos captured at night or of landscapes. A quick shutter speed lets in less light. This is the best way to take images or record videos of subjects moving quickly.
- **EV:** Modify the exposure coefficient. This establishes the amount of light that reaches the camera's sensor. To compensate for low light, increase the exposure.
- **FOCUS:** Adjust the focus setting. To manually adjust the focus, drag the adjustment bar.
- **WB**: Choose the right white balance to ensure that the color range in your photos is accurate. The color temperature is programmable.
- **MIC:** Decide which direction you wish to record at a higher volume for the sound. A USB or Bluetooth microphone can also be used by connecting it to your device in pro video mode.
- **Zoom**: Zoom at a different speed (in pro video mode).

Night mode

When taking a photo in dim light, avoid using the flash. Results can be more consistent and brighter when you use a tripod.

- Select **MORE > NIGHT** from the shooting modes list. You might get sharper images if you set the time that shows at the bottom right of the screen to Max.
- Hold your device steady and press the shutter button until the shooting is finished.

Food mode

Capture food in images with more vivid colors.

- Select **FOOD** from the list of shooting modes. The screen will display a frame, with the surrounding area appearing blurry.
- Drag a corner of the frame to adjust its size. To move the frame, either **tap the desired area or drag it.**
- To change the color temperature, tap **the temperature icon and drag the adjustment bar.**
- To snap a photo, tap **the shutter button.**

Panorama mode

To create a wide scene, take multiple pictures in panorama mode and stitch them together.

- Select **MORE > PANORAMA from the list of shooting modes.**
- Gently **tap and move the gadget in a single direction**. Retain the image in the viewfinder of the camera. Should the preview image be outside of the guide frame or if you do not move the device, the camera will cease taking pictures automatically.
- Press **the stop icon to end the photo shoot.**

Slow motion mode

If you want to watch a video in slow motion, you can designate which parts of your videos should play in slow motion.

- To do this, select **MORE > SLOW MOTION** from the shooting modes list, tap to start recording, and tap again to stop. When you're done, tap the preview thumbnail to bring up the preview screen, where the fast section of the video will automatically be set to play in slow motion. Up to two slow-motion sections will be created based on the video; to edit the slow-motion section, tap and drag the section editing bar to the left or right.

Hyperlapse mode

Take videos of scenes that pass by, like cars or people, and watch them in slow motion.

- Select **MORE > HYPERLAPSE** from the list of shooting modes.
- To choose a frame rate, tap **AUTO.**
  - When you select **AUTO** for the frame rate, the device will automatically modify the frame rate based on how quickly the scene changes.
  - To capture star trails, select and tap the frame rate.
- To begin recording, tap **the recording icon.**
- Press **the stop icon to complete the recording.**

Camera settings

There are so many camera settings and they can be tweaked to give just that which you want when it pertains to pictures and videos. Press the settings button on the preview screen. The shooting mode may prevent you from accessing some options.

Intelligent features

- **Scan text and documents**: The icon will show up when the rear camera identifies a text or document.
- **Scan barcodes**: From the preview screen, configure the device to scan QR codes.
- **Suggested shots**: Utilize the device's ability to identify your subject's position and angle to recommend the best shot composition.
- **Intelligent optimization**
  - **Optimization of quality**: Pick a high-quality choice.
  - **Scene optimizer**: Configure the device to automatically apply the best effect based on the subject or scene and modify the color settings.

Pictures

- **Swipe Shutter button**: Choose an action to carry out when you swipe and hold the camera button at the edge of the screen using the swipe shutter button.
- **Watermark**: When taking photos, include a watermark.
- **Advanced image choices**: Decide how you wish to save the image.
  - **High-efficiency photos**: Use the High-Efficiency Image Format (HEIF) when taking photos.
  - **Picture format for pro mode**: Choose the file format to save images that were taken in pro mode. JPEG files reduce storage requirements and compress images. RAW files (DNG file format) take up more storage space but save images as uncompressed and preserve all of their data for the

best possible image quality. Every image is saved in both DNG and JPG formats when you choose the RAW and JPEG options.

Selfies

- Save selfies as they appear on the preview screen: Configure the device to preserve front-facing camera photos without rotating them.
- Swipe up or down to switch cameras: Activate this feature by using your finger to swipe the preview screen in either direction to change the camera.

Videos

- **Auto FPS:** Adjust the frame rate automatically to make the device record brighter videos in low light.
- **Video stabilization:** Enable anti-shake to minimize or completely remove jagged images that come from the camera shaking while a video is being recorded.
- **Advanced video settings**
  - **Video format**: Choose the format for the video.
  - **High-bitrate videos**: Make videos have a higher bitrate. Use of this feature may result in a larger file size than typical videos.
  - **HDR10+ videos**: These allow you to capture footage with optimal color and contrast in every scene.
  - **Zoom-in microphone**: You can record audio from a closer angle and at a higher volume when you're filming a video.
  - **360 audio recording**: If your Bluetooth headphones have this feature, you can record more immersive 3D sound videos.

General

Tracking auto-focus: Configure the gadget to follow and focus on a chosen subject automatically. The device will focus on a subject you select from the preview screen, regardless of whether the subject is moving or you move the camera.

The following situations could prevent you from tracking a subject:

- The topic is either too large or too little.
- The person moves too much.
- You are photographing in a dimly lit area or the subject is backlit.
- The background and the subject have the same colors or patterns.
- Horizontal patterns, like blinds, are included in the topic.
- The video has a lot of shaking.
- There is a high resolution in the video.
- When using the optical zoom to enlarge or decrease in size.

Grid lines: Show viewfinder guidelines to aid in subject selection and composition.
Location tags: GPS location tags should be added to the image.
- GPS signal strength may drop in places with signal obstructions, such as low-lying areas or spaces between buildings, as well as in unfavorable weather.
- When you upload your photos to the internet, your location might show up in them. You should disable the location tag setting to prevent this.

Shooting methods

- To capture images or record videos, zoom in or out, or adjust the volume, press the **Volume button.**
- **Voice commands**: Use your voice to take photos or record videos.
- **Floating Shutter button**: To take pictures, add another movable button anywhere on the screen.
- **Show palm:** To take selfies or begin recording videos, hold your palm up to the front camera.

Activity

1. Configure the shooting mode on your device.
2. Take pictures with the use of your device.
3. Create an album from the pictures you have taken.
4. Sync your pictures and videos on OneDrive.
5. With the use of the camera settings, tweak the camera settings on your phone.

CHAPTER 13
GALLERY

Gallery is where you get access to all of the images and videos that are saved on your device. You are also able to control pictures and videos in the gallery when you create an album or stories.

- To gain access to the gallery app, all you have to do is tap the Gallery icon on your phone.

How to look at pictures

- Swipe left or right to view other files after opening the Gallery app and choosing an image.

Generative edit

Images can be edited by resizing, moving, or removing people or objects. To replace any missing background, a new one can be created.

- Launch the **Gallery app**, and then **choose a picture.**

- Press the pencil icon and click **Generative.**
- To move or remove anything, simply tap or draw around it. You can drag the tilt adjustment bar to change the tilt.
- You can either tap to remove the selected area or touch and hold it to drag it to the desired location.
- Click "**Generate.**"

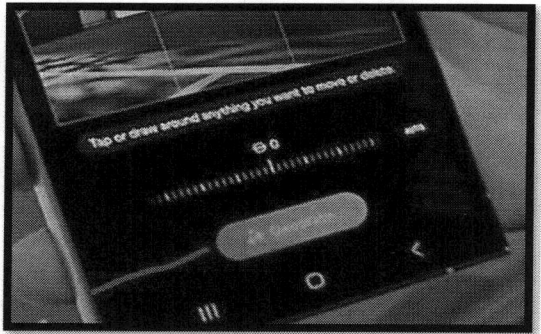

- To save the picture, tap **Done.**

Remastering images

The grainy, blurry, and low-resolution photos can be improved.

- Launch **the Gallery app, and then choose a picture.**
- Press > Remaster. You can view the prior and subsequent.
- Press to store the enhanced picture.

Extracting objects from images

Extract an object by separating it from its surroundings. Once the image has been extracted, you can save it as a sticker or an image and use it in different ways.

- Launch **the Gallery app,** and then **choose a picture.**
- To extract an object, touch and hold it, then choose **an option.**

Cropping enlarged images

- Launch **the Gallery app, and then choose a picture.**
- To save an area, spread your fingers apart and tap **Crop.** A file containing the cropped area will be saved.

Viewing videos

To play a video, launch the Gallery app and choose one. Swipe left or right on the screen to view other files.

- Select **More > Open** in the Video player to access additional playback options.

The brightness and volume can be adjusted by dragging up or down on the left or right side of the playback screen, respectively. Swipe left or right on the playback screen to rewind or fast-forward.

Viewing brighter and clearer videos

When playing videos, turn up the brightness of the screen and boost the vibrancy of the colors.

- Navigate to **Settings > Advanced features**

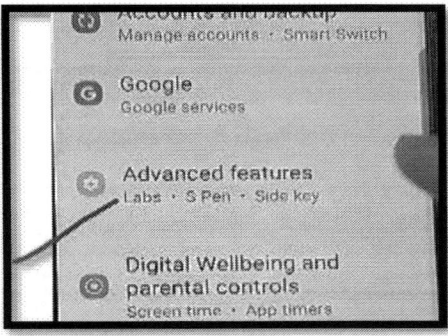

> Video brightness

> Bright

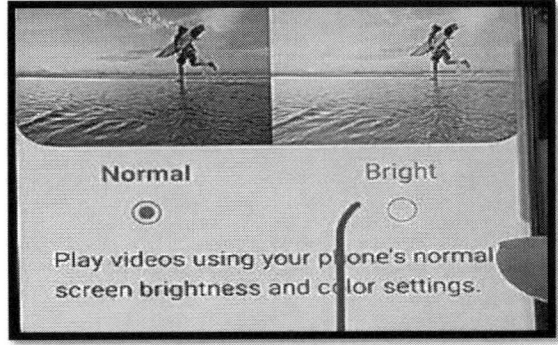

- Only certain apps have this feature.
- The use of this feature will result in higher battery usage.

Editing Your Pictures

Use the editing tools in the Gallery to make your photos look better.

- Select **Pictures from the Gallery.**

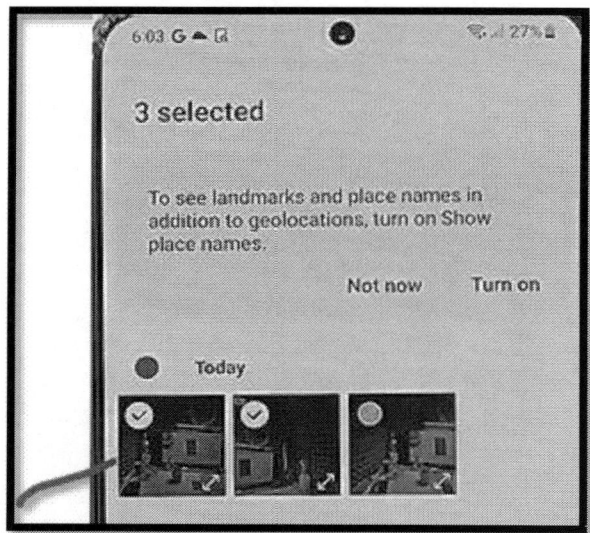

- After tapping an image to view it, you can select one of the following by tapping **Edit:**

  - **Auto adjusts:** Auto adjusts: To enhance the image, make automatic adjustments.
  - **Transform**: Adjust the image's general appearance by rotating, flipping, cropping, or applying other adjustments.
  - **Filters**: Include hue variations.
  - **Tone:** Modify the contrast, exposure, brightness, and other factors.
  - **Decorations:** Add text, stickers, or hand-drawn content as decorations.
  - **Additional choices:** Get access to more editing options.
  - **Revert:** Take back the adjustments made to get the original image back.

Playing Videos

Watch the videos that are saved on your gadget. Videos can be viewed in detail and saved as favorites.

- Select **Pictures from the Gallery.**

- To watch a video, tap **on it.** To see more images or videos, swipe left or right.
    - Click **Add to Favorites** to add the video to your favorites. The Albums tab's Favorites section now includes the video.
    - **Tap More options to view the following features:**
        - **Details:** See and modify the video's metadata.
        - **Launch the video player**: Use the built-in video player to watch this video.
        - **Set as wallpaper:** On the Lock screen set the video as the wallpaper.
        - **Move to Secure Folder**: Add this video to your Secure Folder by moving it there.
- Tap **Play video t**o play the video you have chosen.

Change the brightness of the Video

Improve the video quality to experience richer, more vibrant colors.

- Select an option by selecting **Advanced Features > Video brightness** from the Settings menu.

Edit Video

Modify videos that are saved on your device.

- Select **Pictures from the Gallery.**
- To watch **a video, tap on it.**
- To utilize the following tools, tap **Edit**:
    - **Audio:** Modify the video's volume and add background music.
    - **Play**: See a preview of the cut video.
    - **Trim:** Remove certain video segments.
    - **Transform:** Adjust the video's overall appearance by rotating, flipping, cropping, or applying other effects.
    - **Filters:** Enhance the video's aesthetic appeal.
    - **Tone**: Modify the exposure, contrast, brightness, and other parameters.
    - **Decorations**: Add text, stickers, or hand-drawn content as decorations.
    - **Additional choices:** Get access to more editing options.
    - **Revert:** Take back the modifications made to bring back the original video.

Albums

Launch the **Gallery app, choose an album type, and then tap the Albums > Add icon.**

- **Album**: Make new ones and manually upload pictures and videos.

- **Auto-updating album**: Make albums that compile pictures of the individuals you choose.
- **Group**: Arrange similar albums into a group.
- **Shared album**: Make albums that you can distribute to other people.

Stories

Your device will sort photos and videos and create stories after reading the date and location tags when you take or save them.

- Launch **the Gallery app, and select a story by tapping Stories.** You can use several options by tapping, including altering the title of the story. You can manually create stories by tapping the **More option > Create a story on the stories list.**

How to Take a Screenshot

Take a picture of your display. The Gallery app on your device will launch and automatically create a screenshot album.

- You can press and release **the Side and Volume down keys from any screen.**

Screenshot settings

Change the screenshot's configuration.

- Select **Advanced Features > Screenshots and Screen Recorder from the Settings menu.**
  - **Display toolbar following capture:** Display more options once you've taken a screenshot.
  - **Delete automatically after sharing from the toolbar:** Screenshots that are shared via the screenshot toolbar will automatically be deleted.
  - **Hide the status and navigation bars**: When taking screenshots, make sure the status and navigation bars are hidden.
  - **Forma**t: Select whether you want to save your screenshots as PNG or JPG files.
  - **Save screenshots in** Select where you want to save your screenshots.

Circle to Search

The Galaxy S24 has a feature called Circle to Search that lets you draw a simple gesture with the S Pen or your finger to initiate an automatic search for information about an image or text. Discover how to quickly search for image information on the web, social media, Gallery app, and more by using Circle to Search. With the help of this special feature, you can quickly search the web for interesting items within an image or text without having to switch between apps or type out your search terms. Simply circle the item or text of interest with your finger or an S-pen, and the search will start on its own. Any app that supports screen capture can use this feature.

- Navigate to **Settings > Tap Display.**
- Press the **Navigation bar.**
- Turn on **Circle to Search.**

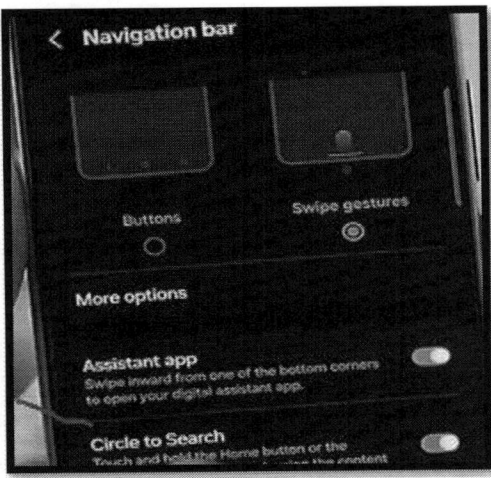

You can do an internet search by simply circling an object of interest in an image with an internet connection, your Galaxy phone, and a few simple steps.

- Holding **the home key, tap on it.**
- To circle or tap **the object of interest, use your finger or an S-pen.**
- When you take your finger or S-pen off the phone's screen, the web search will start.

Deleting images or videos

- To delete an image, video, or story, launch **the Gallery app**, touch and hold the image or video you would like to delete, and then select **Delete.**

Using the recycle bin feature

When you delete photos or videos, they will be momentarily kept in the recycle bin. After a specific amount of time, the files will be removed.

- Open the Gallery app, and select **More > Recycle bin,** to view the files in the recycle bin. If you would like to bring back any file from the recycle bin, tap **Edit, choose the files you want to restore**, and then tap **Restore.**

AR Zone

You can access AR-related features at AR Zone. Select a feature, then record amusing images or videos.

Launching AR Zone

Launch AR Zone using one of the following methods:

- Select **AR ZONE** from the list of shooting modes in the Camera app by tapping **MORE**.

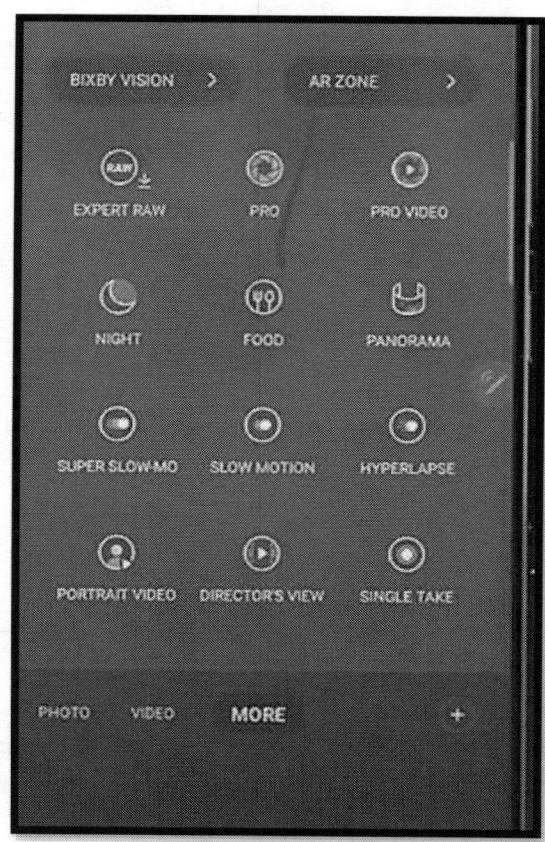

- Launch the **AR Zone app** if you have added it to the app icon on the Apps screen.

AR Emoji Studio

Make your emojis and enjoy utilizing them in a variety of applications.

- Open AR Zone, and then select **AR Emoji Studio.**

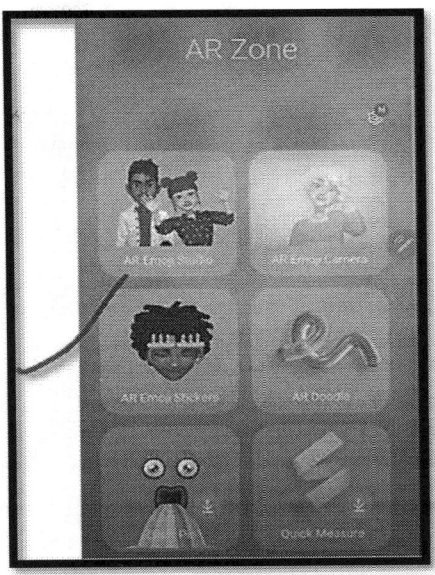

- You may select an already-made emoji. After choosing an emoji with a swipe to the left or right, tap the forward-pointing arrow.

To create your emoticon, either choose an image or take a selfie.

Selecting an AR emoji to use

- Choose your desired emoji by tapping on it on the AR Emoji Studio home screen.

Deleting AR emojis

- To delete emojis, select them on the **AR Emoji Studio main screen** by tapping and then tapping **Delete.**

Syncing AR emojis

Once you have logged into the same Samsung account on each device, you can access your AR emojis across all of them. The Sync with Samsung Cloud switch can be toggled on or off from the AR Emoji Studio main screen by selecting **More > Settings.**

Creating an AR emoji short video and decorating your device with it

Emojis can be used to create a brief video that you can use as a call background image or wallpaper.

- To make a video, choose **Create video, Alarm background, Call screen, or Lock screen from the AR Emoji Studio main screen.**

The saved videos are viewable in the Gallery.

Creating your contact profile with an AR emoji

Make use of an emoji as your Contacts app and Samsung account profile picture. You can make your expressions or select from a variety of stances.

- To choose an emoji, tap **Profile on the main screen of AR Emoji Studio**.
- Press **to record your facial expression or choose a desired position.**
- Click "**Done**" > "**Save.**"

AR Emoji Stickers

Stickers with emoji actions and expressions will be generated automatically when you create AR emojis. Additionally, you can alter the background and expression to make your stickers. Emoji stickers can be utilized for messaging purposes or on social media platforms.

Creating your stickers

- Select **AR Emoji Stickers** after opening the AR Zone.
- On the sticker list, tap **the add icon at the top.**
- After making any necessary edits, select **Save**. At the top of the stickers list, you can see the stickers you have created.

Using AR emoji stickers in chats

You can use your emoji stickers on social media or in text messages to participate in conversations. The Messages app's emoji stickers can be used in the ways shown below.

- Tap the Samsung Keyboard while writing a message in the Messages app.
- Press **the emoticon symbol.**
- Choose **an emoji sticker from your library.** You are then going to insert the emoji sticker.

AR Doodle (Record videos with the AR feature)

Make amusing videos in which you virtually write or draw on the faces of people, pets (dogs and cats), or anyplace else. When a face or space is detected by the camera, the doodles on the face will move with the face, and the doodles in the space will stay in place regardless of camera movement.

- Open AR Zone, and then select **AR Doodle**. The recognition area will show up on the screen once the subject has been identified by the camera.

- **In the recognition area, write or draw.**
  - You can also write or draw outside of the recognition area if you switch to the rear camera.
  - You can record yourself doodling if you **tap and start drawing.**
- To capture a video, tap **the record icon.**
- To end the video recording, tap the stop button. In the Gallery, you can **view and share the video.**

Music Share

If you have a Bluetooth speaker that is currently connected to your phone, you can allow another person to use it by enabling the Music Sharing option on your phone. It is also possible to listen to the same song on both your Galaxy Buds as well as another person's Galaxy Buds at the same time. Only devices that support the Music Sharing function will have access to this feature.

Sharing a Bluetooth speaker

You can get to hear music on your phone and your friend's phone with the use of your Bluetooth speaker.

- Ensure that your phone and also your Bluetooth speaker are connected.
- On your phone, open **Settings, touch Connections > Bluetooth > Menu icons (three dots) > Advanced settings then touch the Music Share toggle to have it**

turned on. You can also make use of some extra features like configuring those you would like to share your device with by touching **Music Share**.

- Grab your friend's phone, and choose your speaker from the list of Bluetooth devices.
- On your phone, allow for the connection of the request. Your speaker will then be shared. When you also play music with the use of your friend's phone, the music being played via your phone will be paused.

Listening to music together with Galaxy Buds

It is possible to share the experience of listening to music on your phone with a friend by using both of your earbuds.

This functionality is exclusive to the Galaxy Buds family of headphones.

- Be sure that each phone and pair of Buds have been connected.
- Grab your friend's phone, open **Settings, touch Connections > Bluetooth > menu icon (three dots) > Advanced settings then touch the Music Share toggle to have it turned on.** You can also make use of extra features like configuring those you would like to share your device with by touching Music Share.
- On your phone, open **the notification panel and touch the Media output**.
- Touch **Music Share and choose the Bud belonging to your friend** from the detected list of devices.
- On your friend's phone, allow the connection request. When music is being played via your phone, you would be able to listen to it with the use of both Buds.

Activity

1. View videos and edit pictures on your device.
2. Adjust the brightness of the video.
3. Navigate through albums and stories on your device.
4. Take a screenshot on your device.
5. Delete an image or video on your device.
6. What is the function of the AR zone and AR Doodle?

CHAPTER 14

THE CALENDAR AND CLOCK APPS

As you manage your time well, systematic planning and scheduling can help you succeed. Learn how to use this straightforward and effective Samsung Calendar app to manage your schedule. With its many features for keeping your diary organized, you can meet all of your needs and maintain consistency in your routine. You can sync all of your calendars in one location by connecting the Calendar app to your different online accounts.

Basic navigation in the Calendar app

The navigation of Samsung Calendar is superior to that of Google Calendar, even though Samsung's default setting is not to track the information about your events. If you want to view the calendar by the year, the month, the week, or the day, you can press the hamburger menu like you would on Google Calendar. What you do not get, however, is the three-day view that is available on Google Calendar (but Google Calendar does not have a year view either). In addition, the search function is located at the very bottom of the menu, where it appears to be an afterthought.

There will be occasions when you need to search for information, such as when someone's birthday is or when a conference is planned to take place. It is inconvenient that the search function is located below the scroll. Yet if you look at the calendar itself, you can see that the month and the year are written at the very top of the grid. You can only view the month on Google Calendar, and the information it provides is only instructive. There is no effect caused by selecting it. This implies that if you want to look back at something you've done in the past or flick ahead on your agenda, you will need to navigate from page to page. That is a time-consuming operation if you are verifying a date that is several years in the future. And the fact that Google Calendar doesn't offer a year view doesn't make things any simpler there either. If it's not going to be happening anytime soon, as far as Google is concerned, there's no reason for you to know about it. When you select the month and year at the very top of the Samsung Calendar, you will be presented with a list of the months and years that follow.

Start with your calendar settings

When you initially turn on the device, you will be given the option to link it to your calendar by selecting one of the following four accounts: your Samsung account, Exchange (Outlook), Google, or Microsoft. Your already established schedules will be synchronized once you have entered both your email address and your password.

How to change calendar settings

You can change the settings on your Calendar app so that they are more suitable for your needs and easier for you to make use of.

- Open the **Calendar app** and touch the **Menu button (three horizontal lines)**
- Touch the **Settings icon**.

- First day of the week: You are free to choose any one of the seven days that make up a week to serve as the beginning day of the week.
- Alternate calendar: The Samsung Calendar provides users with a total of five different calendars to choose from. There is the lunar calendar of Korea, China, Vietnam, the Hijri calendar, and the Shamsi calendar.
- Show week numbers: With this option, you'll be able to add a number to your calendar that provides you with information about the number of weeks.
- Hide declined event: with this option, you can hide the schedules you have denied.
- Highlight short events: with this option, you can do in a very short amount of time in highlight events.

How to create events

With the use of the calendar, you can choose to create events so that you won't forget about the activities you have ahead.

- Open the **Calendar app**, and then choose the date you would like to include the date you wish to add to the schedule.

- Touch **the + icon > modify the Title of the event**.

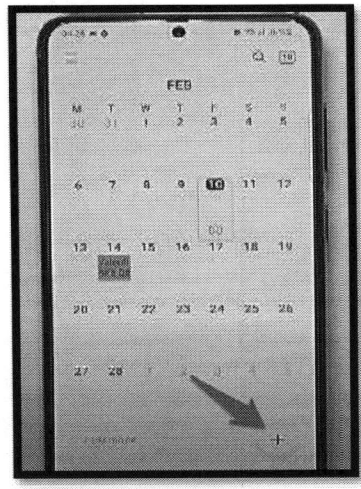

- If you would like to take note of the duration of the event, configure the **Start and End date and time**.
- If need be, you can choose to insert the **Location and Alert types** and also various configurations and touch the **Save button** to have the event saved.

How to delete or edit an event

Events created can be deleted when the event has already taken place or they can be modified if there is a need for that to be done.

- Touch **the date of the YOU would like to either delete or edit and hold the event**.

- Touch **Delete or Edit to modify** the event in detail.

How to link external accounts added to synced calendars

You can have your external accounts linked to your calendar this way you can keep tabs on all of your plans in one piece.

- Open the **Calendar app** and touch the **Menu (three horizontal lines)**.
- Choose an **email and touch on the accounts** you would like to link.
- Touch on **Sync now**.

How to share your calendar

You can share your calendar with friends, family, and most especially co-workers. With this, you can easily choose a particular time to collaborate with your coworkers to work on a piece with the new advent of collaboration on the cloud such as working on a Google document together.

- Choose the preferred date you would like to share touch and hold on to the specific event.
- Touch **Share > Choose Share as a Calendar file or text**.

Reminder (Receiving notifications for to-do items)

Set up recollections for tasks and get alerts based on the parameters you establish.

- Connect to a mobile or Wi-Fi network to get more accurate notifications.
- The GPS feature needs to be enabled to use location reminders. Depending on the model, location reminders might not be available.

Starting Reminder

- Select **More > Reminders** when the Calendar app is open. The Reminder app icon will be added to the Apps screen, and the Reminder screen will display.

Creating reminders

- Launch the **Reminder application.**
- Select the **Add icon**; fill in the information, and select **Save.**

Restoring reminders

Return completed reminders to their original state.

- Select **Completed under More options** on the list of reminders.

- To restore, choose **a reminder and hit Restore**. You will receive another reminder and the reminders will be added to your list.

Deleting reminders

- Choose **a reminder and tap Delete to remove it.** Touch and hold **a reminder, select the reminders you want to delete, and then tap Delete** to remove multiple reminders.

Voice Recorder

Play or record audio files

- Start the **Voice Recorder application.**
- To begin recording, tap **the recording icon.** Talk into the microphone.

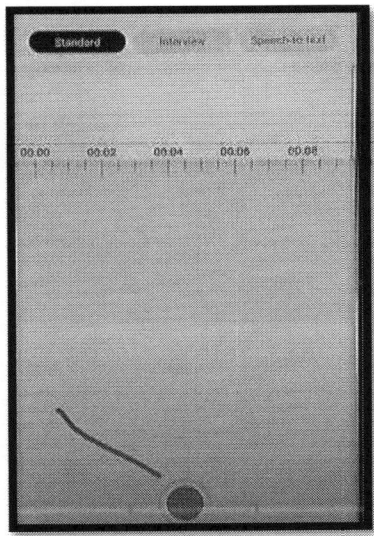

- To stop recording, tap **the stop recording icon**.
- Click to add a bookmark while recording audio.
- To end the recording, ta**p the stop recording icon.**
- After naming the file, click **Save.**

Transcribing voice recordings

Transform voice recordings into text on the screen, and then review summaries. The converted text can also be translated into other languages.

- Choose **a voice recording.**

- To choose your preferred language, tap **Transcribe**. Click **Add Languages** to download a language pack if the language you want isn't on the list.
- Select **Transcribe.**
  - Press **Summary** to view the summary and keywords.
  - To view the translated text, tap **and choose a language.**
  - Press **More options > Transcribe** once more to transcribe the recording into a different language.

Play selected voice recordings

You have the option to mute or unmute specific sound sources in interview recordings when reviewing them.

- Choose **an audio clip recorded while in interview mode.**

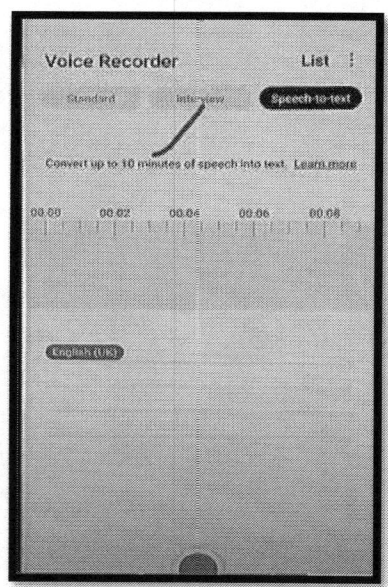

- Press the corresponding direction of the sound you want to mute to turn it off. Both the **icon and the sound will become muted.**

Gaming Hub

Your downloaded games from the Play Store and Galaxy Store are gathered in one location by Gaming Hub. Select your desired game by opening the Gaming Hub app. The Gaming Hub screen will automatically display games that have been downloaded from the Play Store and Galaxy Store. Press **My Games> More options > Add games** if your games aren't there.

Removing a game from the Gaming Hub

- Touch and hold **a game after tapping My Games, and then select Remove from Gaming Hub.**

Changing the performance mode

The game's performance mode is modifiable.

- Launch the Gaming Hub app, and choose **your preferred mode by tapping More > Game Booster > Game Optimization.**
- **Performance**: The goal of this is to provide you with optimal gaming performance. Use of this mode may cause your device to overheat due to higher battery usage.
- **Standard**: This strikes a balance between battery life and performance.
- **Battery saver**: When playing games, this preserves battery life.

Game Booster

With Game Booster, you can enjoy a more enjoyable gaming experience. While playing games, Game Booster can be used. **Tap the navigation bar to bring up the Game Booster panel while you're playing.**

- To reveal the navigation bar, drag it up from the bottom of the screen if it's hidden. Open the notification panel, and then tap **Tap to Open Game Booster** if you have the navigation bar set to use swipe gestures.

As long as the navigation bar is configured for swipe gestures, you can use it to open the Game Booster panel. To enable navigation gestures during gameplay, go to **Settings > Block during a game on the Game Booster panel and tap the switch.** The options available might change based on the game. If the temperature rises above a predetermined point, game performance might be restricted to regulate the device's temperature.

Clock

Alarm

To set one-time or recurring alarms and select how to be notified, use the Alarm tab.

- Click on **Add alarm from Clock.**
- You can choose any of the following options to set up an alarm:

  - **Time**: Decide on an alarm time.
  - **Day**: Select the days that this alarm will sound.

- **Name of alarm**: Type a name for the alarm here.
- **Alarm sound**: Select the sound to be played, and then adjust the volume by dragging the slider.
- **Vibration**: Select if you want the alarm to vibrate or not.
- **Snooze**: Permit dozing off. When you're sleeping, set the alarm's interval and repeat settings.
- To save the alarm, tap **Save.**

Note that you can select **More options > Set Sleep mode schedule** to add your sleep schedule, set up a bedtime reminder, and have your device automatically go into sleep mode.

Delete an alarm

An alarm that you have created can be removed.

- Touch and hold **an alarm from the clock.**
- Press **Delete.**

Alert settings

Whether the Sound mode is set to Mute or vibrate, you can configure the device to vibrate for timers and alarms.

- Select **More Options > Settings from the Clock menu.**
- To activate the feature, press **Silence** alarms when the system sound is off.

Alarm settings

Notifications regarding impending alarms are sent to you.

- Press **More options > Settings from the Clock menu.**
- You can select how many minutes before an upcoming alarm, by tapping the **Upcoming alarm notification.**

World Clock

You can monitor the time in several cities across the world with the World Clock.

- Select **World Clock from Clock.**
- Click "**Add city.**"
- To rotate the globe, drag it, tap the desired city, and then select **Add.**
  - Touch and hold a city to remove it, and then select **Delete.**

Time zone converter

To find out the local times in the other cities on your list, set a time in one of the cities on your World Clock list.

- Select **World Clock from Clock.**
- Select the **Time zone converter under More options.**
- To switch to a different city, tap Menu.
    - o Tap **Add City** to add a city to the list.
- To set a time, swipe the clock's hours, minutes, and period (AM or PM). The other cities' local times are automatically updated.
    - Press **Reset t**o get the clock back to the current time.

Weather settings

Display meteorological data on your global timepiece.

- Select **World Clock from Clock.**
- To turn on or off weather information, tap **More options > Settings > Show weather.**
- To convert between Fahrenheit and Celsius, tap **Temperature.**

Stopwatch

You can time events to the nearest hundredth of a second with the stopwatch.

- Press **Stopwatch from Clock.**
- To start timing, tap **Start.**
    - o Press **Lap** to record your lap times.
- To stop the timing, tap **Stop.**
    - After stopping the timer, tap **Resume to resume timing.**
    - Tap **Reset** to set the Stopwatch back to zero.

Timer

For a maximum of 99 hours, 59 minutes, and 59 seconds, set a countdown timer.

- Select **Timer from Clock.**
- To set the timer, use the keypad and tap Hours, Minutes, and Seconds.
- To start the timer, tap **Start.**
    - Tap **Pause** to put the Timer on hold. Press **Resume proceeding.**
    - Tap **Delete** to end and restart the timer.

Preset timer

Set a preset timer and save it.

- Select **Timer > More options > Add preset timer from the Clock menu.**
- Establish **the timer name and countdown duration.**
- To save the timer, tap **Add.**
    - Select **More options > Edit preset timers** to make changes to a saved preset timer.

Timer options

There is an option to customize the Timer.

- Select **Timer from Clock.**
- Select **Settings from the More options menu.**
    - Sound: Select one of the timer's built-in sounds or add your own.
    - Vibration: Turn on the timer's vibration feature.
    - Display mini timer: When the Clock app is minimized, the timer will appear in a pop-up window.

Activity

1. Configure the various settings on your calendar to your taste.
2. Create events on your calendar.
3. Edit an event you have created earlier.
4. Link accounts added to the synced calendar.
5. Share your calendar with your friends or colleagues.
6. Configure the clock so you can tell the time and know what the time is in other parts of the world.

CHAPTER 15

SAMSUNG DEX

Samsung DeX lets you turn your phone or tablet into a PC, ushering in a new era of mobile-powered desktop computing. The finest aspect? It's cost-free. Many of the most recent Samsung Galaxy mobile devices come pre-installed with the DeX software platform, so all you need to get started is a monitor, an HDMI adapter, and some accessories. You can even use DeX wirelessly if your Smart TV or monitor supports Miracast. With the Samsung DeX software platform, you can use your tablet or smartphone like a desktop computer. Virtually every flagship smartphone released by Samsung since 2017 is compatible with it, beginning with the Galaxy S8 and continuing through the Galaxy S24, S24+, and S24 Ultra models from this year as well as the newest foldable flagship, the Galaxy Z Fold5. Some Samsung Galaxy tablets support DeX as well, such as the rugged Tab Active4 Pro and the Tab S9. DeX can be used on a connected monitor with an external keyboard and mouse, or directly on the screen of larger tablets when paired with a keyboard case.

Which Dex adapter is best?

For Samsung DeX and Samsung DeX on PC, Samsung provides a variety of cables and accessories. The benefits of each cable and adapter vary based on where and how the platform is used. The DeX cable enables you to effortlessly connect your device to the conventional HDMI port on your monitor. With its 1.4 meters of length, you can use it with nearly any type of monitor arrangement. If you can leave the DeX cable attached to your monitor and you intend to use DeX primarily in one place, then that cable is perfect for you. It's frequently utilized in workplace hot-desking situations, where employees simply stop by, plug in their phones, and get to work. The DeX multiport adapter provides the greatest flexibility when using DeX and has a full range of ports. You have a USB 3.0 port to connect a keyboard or mouse, a USB-C port to connect the charging cable for your phone, and an HDMI port to connect the HDMI cable to your monitor. The multiport adapter is small enough to fit in a pocket.

If you have a USB-C monitor, a USB-C to USB-C cable is a great choice. The device is connected to one end, and the monitor is directly connected to the other. The ability of your monitor to serve as a hub for connecting your wired keyboard and mouse is another benefit of using USB-C cables and monitors. Additionally, it can maintain the battery life of your device in DeX mode. If you have a more recent laptop with USB-C ports, you can also use a USB-C to USB-C cable for DeX on PC. Alternatively, you can use a standard USB-C to USB-A charging cable for wired DeX on your PC. It's likely that you already have one for charging gadgets. Simply unplug the wall charger's USB cord and insert it into a USB port on your Mac or PC. Furthermore, Samsung has released a Smart Keyboard designed specifically for DeX in addition to these adapters. The Bluetooth keyboard features function keys for quickly switching between connectivity on your PC, tablet, and Galaxy smartphone in addition to a dedicated key to start DeX instantly.

Controlling devices and starting Samsung Dex

Wired connections to external displays

An HDMI adapter (USB) can be used to connect your mobile device to an external display.

HDMI to Type-C connector)

Use only the official, Samsung-provided accessories that are compatible with Samsung DeX. The warranty does not cover malfunctions or performance issues brought on by using accessories that are not officially supported.

- Attach a mobile device to an HDMI adapter.
- Attach an HDMI cable to the HDMI port on a TV or monitor.
- On the screen of your mobile device, select **Start**. The Samsung DeX screen will display on the connected TV or monitor without altering the screen on your mobile device.

Wirelessly connecting to a TV

By wirelessly connecting your mobile device to a TV, you can use Samsung DeX.

- Open the notification panel on your mobile device, swipe down, and then tap **(DeX).**
- From the list of detected devices, choose **a TV a**nd press **Start Now**. Certain TVs can only be identified when their screen mirroring feature is activated.
- Accept the request if the TV displays the connection request window.
- To finish the connection, adhere to the on-screen directions. The TV will display the Samsung DeX screen once they are connected.

Controlling the Samsung DeX screen

Controlling with an external keyboard and mouse

A wireless keyboard and mouse are an option.

- The mouse pointer can be configured to move from the external display to the screen of the mobile device. Turn it on by opening **Settings, choosing Samsung DeX > Mouse and trackpad, and then choosing the Flow pointer to the phone screen switch.**

- The screen of the mobile device also allows you to utilize the external keyboard as well.

Using your mobile device as a touchpad

- Your mobile device can function as a touchpad. You can tap the navigation bar on your mobile device. Open the notification panel, selects **Use your phone as a touchpad, and then confirms that the navigation bar is configured to use swipe gestures.**

Note

- You can view the gestures that can be used with the touchpad by **double-tapping on it.**
- If the front cover of your mobile device is removable, open it to use your device as a touchpad. Proper operation of the touchpad may be impeded if the front cover is closed.
- Hit the **Side button or double-tap the screen** to turn it back on if your mobile device's screen goes dark.

Using the screen keyboard

Without connecting an external keyboard, a screen keyboard will automatically appear on the screen of your mobile device when you enter text to send messages, take notes, or carry out other tasks.

Using Samsung DeX

Utilize the features on your mobile device in a computer-like interface. You can run multiple apps at once to multitask. Additionally, you can view the status and notifications on your mobile device.

Kindly take note of the following;

- The connected device may have an impact on the Samsung DeX screen layout.
- During Samsung DeX startup or shutdown, open apps might be closed.
- With Samsung DeX, some apps or features might not be accessible.
- Use the display settings on the connected TV or monitor to change the screen's parameters.
- Tap the status bar, choose **Media Output,** and then pick a device to adjust the audio output.

Using Samsung DeX and mobile devices simultaneously

You can use different apps on your mobile device and the external display at the same time when using Samsung DeX. For example, you can use Messenger to have a conversation with a friend while viewing a video on a connected TV or monitor. Open an app to use on the Samsung DeX screen on the TV or monitor that is connected. Then, open a different app on your mobile device.

Locking the Samsung DeX screen

- Choose **More options > Lock DeX** if you wish to lock both the Samsung DeX screen and the screen of your mobile device while using Samsung DeX. You are unable to use the Side button to lock the screens of your mobile device and Samsung DeX while using the app.

Activity

1. What is Samsung Dex?
2. Configure the Samsung Dex.
3. Connect your phone or monitor to your phone with the use of Samsung Dex.

CHAPTER 16

SAMSUNG WALLET (SAMSUNG PAY)

Samsung Wallet

Make use of different features in Samsung Wallet. Payment can be made and identity can also be verified with the use of your biometric data, view tickets or boarding passes and so much more. You can verify your biometric data with Samsung Pass and also verify your identity with the use of services that need your login or your personal information. You can include boarding passes and tickets for sports, movies, and a lot more to gain access and also make use of them in just one place.

Digital key

Connect the digital key to your car's ignition system and use your phone to open and close the doors and start the engine. To get started with digital key registration, download your vehicle's digital key app or follow the instructions provided in the manufacturer-sent communication (email or text). Then, to finish the registration, follow the on-screen directions presented to you on both your car's navigation screen and your phone's Samsung Wallet screen. **It is worth noting that;**

- This feature might not be available based on the region or model.
- If you would like to make use of this feature, your vehicle must offer support for the digital key feature. Check with the manufacturer of your vehicle for support on the digital key.
- Your phone alone saves the registered digital key, if the phone is changed; the digital key must be re-registered again.
- Certain vehicles might not be available based on the vehicle. Check with the manufacturer of your vehicle for more information.

Making use of the digital key with the NFC feature

Tap the NFC antenna area of the phone with the use of the digital key that has been registered with the door of the vehicle. The door will then either lock or unlock. When you position the phone on the wireless charging pad of the vehicle, the digital key will be authenticated after which you can proceed to start the vehicle with the use of the start button.

- To make use of this feature, the phone as well as the vehicle must offer support for the NFC feature.

- To switch on the feature of the NFC on the phone, **Open Settings, touch Connections > NFC and contactless payment then touch the Switch to have it turned on**.

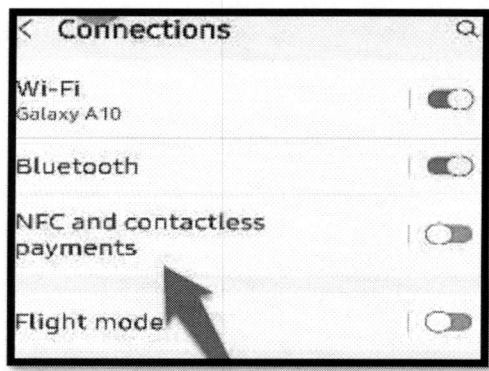

- If you would like to search for the location of the wireless charging pad and ascertain the specific door of your vehicle that offers support for NFC, refer to the user manual of your vehicle.

Make use of the digital key with the Ultra-wideband (UWB) (Galaxy S24 Ultra, Galaxy S24+)

When you approach the car while holding your phone, the door will unlock; when you pull away, it will lock again. Once the digital key has been verified upon entry, you can press the ignition switch to begin driving.

- To make use of this unique feature, the phone and vehicle must offer support for both the Bluetooth and the UWB features. Open Settings, touch Connections then touch the Bluetooth switch and the Ultra-wideband (UWB) switch to have them turned on.
- If the vehicle offers support for both the NFC and UWB features, you can decide the preferred method you want.
- The UWB feature might not be available based on the region.
- The door lock and unlock methods might vary based on the type of vehicle. Check with the manufacturer of your vehicle for more information.
- When you make use of this feature it will increase the consumption of your battery.

Note that you can choose to delete the registered digital from your phone.

- Open the Samsung Wallet application then touch the registered **dial key > touch the three dots (menu icon) > Delete**.

Samsung Pay

Samsung Pay is a digital wallet and mobile payment service developed by Samsung Electronics that enables customers to buy things with their Samsung smartphones and other compatible devices. The service is compatible with contactless payments made by near-field communications (NFC) as well as magnetic stripe-only payment terminals through the use of magnetic secure transmission (MST) in certain devices. It also works for paying bills in India. On August 20, 2015, the service was introduced in South Korea, and on September 28, 2015, it was introduced in the United States.

- To make payments with the use of Samsung Pay, the device might require a connection to either a Wi-Fi or mobile network based on the region.
- This feature might not be available based on the carrier or model.
- The processes for the basic setup and registration of cards might be different based on the carrier or model.
- If you do not have the Samsung Pay app on your device, you can gain access to Samsung Pay from the Samsung Wallet app.

Setting up Samsung Pay

When you execute this application for the first time or you restart the application after you have performed a data reset, follow the instructions on the screen to complete the basic setup.

- Open the **Samsung Pay application**.
- Sign in to your **Samsung account** then read and agree with the terms and conditions.

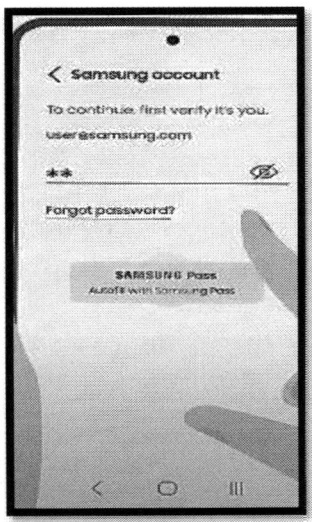

- Create a **fingerprint ID** and a personal identification number for use in making purchases.

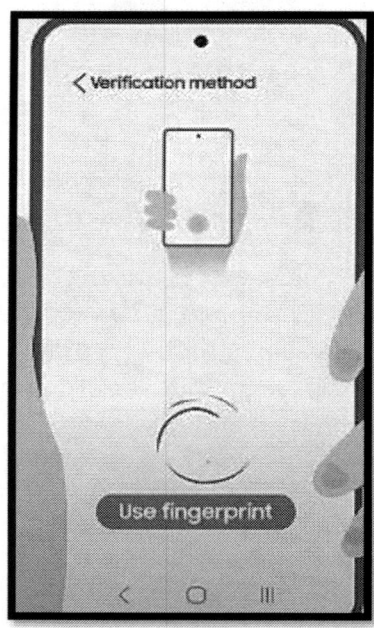

This PIN will be used to authenticate you whenever you make a purchase or use other features within Samsung Pay.

Registering cards

Open the Samsung Pay application and follow the instructions on the screen to complete the registration of your card.

Making payments

- Move the image of a card located at the lower part of the screen upwards. As an alternative, you can also open the **Samsung Pay app**. Then on the list of cards, swipe to the left or the right and choose a card to make use of.
- Scan your fingerprint or insert the payment PIN you configured.
- Tap the back of your device to the card reader. When the card reader recognizes the information on the card, the payment will be processed immediately.

Note that payments might not be processed based on the network connection. The method of verification for payments might also vary based on the card readers.

Canceling payments

Simply return to the location where you originally made the payment to get it canceled.

Swipe left or right on the list of cards to choose the one you just used. Canceling a payment is as simple as following the on-screen prompts.

Use gift cards with Samsung

Gift cards are often well received. You can buy gift cards from a variety of retailers and then spend them from within the app if you use Samsung Pay. This eliminates the need to bring a physical deck of gift cards with you wherever you go. Additionally, there is no limit to the number of gift cards that can be added to your Samsung Pay account. You also have the option to load a real gift card that you have already purchased.

Purchase a gift card for yourself

If you are in the mood to treat yourself, you may use Samsung Pay to purchase a gift card that you can then spend on anything you like.

- Locate and open **Samsung Pay > touch Menu > touch the Gift card store**.
- Make use of the search bar to locate the gift card you prefer. Or, you can check the gift cards available by swiping up and down on the screen.
- Choose your preferred gift card and choose your preferred dollar amount.
- Touch **For me > Touch Add to Cart** and on the following page, tap **Check Out**.
- Ensure Samsung Pay is chosen at the top, and touch **Pay with Samsung Pay at the lower part of the screen**.

- You may additionally need to tap your IRIS or PIN before entering the necessary security information. Simply placing your finger on the fingerprint scanner on your phone will activate the fingerprint security that you have set up.
- Your acquisition will be validated, and the gift card you selected will become accessible through Samsung Pay. In addition to that, you will receive it in an email. You can begin making purchases with the gift card at this time.

Purchase a gift card for a friend

Never again should you question what to get someone for their birthday. Using Samsung Pay, you may purchase a digital gift card and then give it to a friend by email.

- You can buy gift cards by navigating to **Samsung Pay**, opening it, tapping the **Menu button (which looks like three horizontal lines)**, and then tapping the **Gift card store.**
- Make use of the search box to locate the gift card that you are looking for. Swiping up and down will bring you to a list of gift cards that are currently available.
- Choose **the gift card you want**, and then choose the amount you want it to be in dollars. After that, select **"For a Friend,"** and then **enter their details**. To add something to your shopping cart, touch **Add to Cart.**
- On the page that follows, touch **Check Out**. Ensure that Samsung Pay is chosen at the top then touch **Pay with Samsung Pay** at the lower part of the screen.
- You may additionally need to tap your IRIS or PIN before entering the necessary security information. Simply placing your finger on the fingerprint scanner on your phone will activate the fingerprint security that you have set up.
- If your friend makes use of Samsung Pay, the gift card will automatically be delivered to their Samsung Pay app. In addition to that, they will receive it in an email.
- If you purchased a person who does not use Samsung Pay, the recipient of the gift card will get an email with the gift card attached. By following the link that is supplied to them and printing out a copy of the gift card, they will be able to redeem their gift card. They also have the option to download Samsung Pay on a phone that is compatible with it.

Activity

1. What is a Samsung wallet and what is it used for?
2. Make use of gift cards with Samsung.

CHAPTER 17

HOW TO EDIT VIDEOS WITH THE INSHOT APP

Taking pictures is one method that people may ensure they will always remember an important moment. We can reflect on the challenging and successful moments of our journey through the use of photographs. You can enrich your images with the help of some amazing photo editing software. While photographs evoke the same feelings, videos have a distinct impact. Videos present the happenings as they were at the time they were recorded as well as what took place behind the scenes. We get out our mobile devices and begin recording everything we can think of. The art and elegance of video editing are something that comes along with these videos. At this time in history, it has become a delightful hobby to be able to create and edit videos wherever you are. It is an important route to take, whether for personal or professional reasons. There is a plethora of software designed to edit videos that you may download on your mobile device. In this manner, you would not need to purchase an expensive laptop to configure and edit your videos. All you need is a smartphone, an imaginative mind, and a fair degree of expertise.

The InShot app is a video editing and creation application that is simple to use. It also offers a pleasant interface. Your videos can be trimmed, cropped, sped up, or edited with filters with this application. It was created to help you put the finishing touches on your uploads more effectively. The video editing application InShot is ideal for those who place a greater emphasis on keeping their videos as simple as possible. It possesses sophisticated editing tools in addition to an easy-to-use UI. With all of these features, the InShot app is the perfect location to rapidly get started in the world of video editing.

Download the InShot App

To download the application, visit **Google Play Store > In the search box type InShot** and when the app appears on the screen tap it to begin downloading.

Add Photos and Videos to your video

Putting together a video is a piece of cake when you use the Inshot app; all you need to get started is a collection of photographs or videos to edit.

- Start by opening the **Inshot app and selecting the video** that you want to modify before you can add any photographs or videos to your film. You'll be able to navigate through all of your photographs and videos and add any that you like to your video from this window.

- After that, tap t**he three vertical lines in the lower-right area of the screen** to access the **"Photos & Videos" menu**. After you have decided on the video you want to modify, select the **"Photos & Videos"** option from the menu.
- To finish, select **'Add Pictures & Videos' from the menu**.

Import other Photos and Videos

The Inshot app makes it incredibly easy to create videos from start to finish. The first thing that needs to be done is to import images and videos from your personal computer. Make any necessary adjustments to your content before you publish it, once you have reviewed it. When you are finished, you have the option of storing the videos and photographs on inshot.com in a gallery or on individual pages dedicated to the videos and photos. There is no reason for you to delay getting started generating videos right away.

Arrange Clips

On the timeline, the clips are presented in the order that they were put into the video, which was their original order. But, you can adjust their position at any time.

- To access the mode for rearranging the video clips, simply **tap and hold any video clip in the timeline**. After that, reposition the **clip thumbnail by dragging it to a new location**.

Delete clip

To remove a specific segment from the video, tap on the segment first to select it. You will notice that there is a white border surrounding it. After that, select the Delete tool from the bottom toolbar by tapping on it.

Resize video

You might want to turn a landscape video into a portrait one or vice versa, or you might want to publish a video that you published to Instagram Story on YouTube. Both of these things are possible. When this occurs, the videos will have a different aspect ratio than usual. Thus, you should alter the videos' canvas sizes rather than starting from the beginning to create them again. This is not the best method, since it may result in your video having blank borders or the video being cropped in some way. Tap the Canvas option within the InShot video editor, and then choose the desired aspect ratio from the list of available choices.

- To zoom in and out of the movie, use the **pinching motion or your thumb and index finger**. If you want to add the new video size to the currently selected clip, tap **the icon with a single check mark**; if you want to apply it to all clips, tap **the icon with two checkmarks**.

Change Background

If your video has a white background after you have modified the aspect ratio, you can have it filled with color or include a blur effect. If you would like to get this done,

- Touch the **Background toll in the toolbar** and choose **your preferred color or effect from the options made available**.

Video cropping

You have the option of cropping the video to the needed dimensions if you do not desire the video to have a background. To accomplish this, use the Crop tool from the toolbar. Select a dimension from the available options, and then reposition the selection box such that it encompasses the desired space. As was to be expected, you will miss out on certain parts of the video.

Add sound or music video

To add some music as background to your videos, you can either tap the note icon or select the Music tab. There is a music library available within the InShop app. You can pick and select from a variety of tunes and a variety of albums. You can also select songs from iTunes or the music folder on your computer. There are a variety of sound effects that correspond to different themes. Some of them are instrumental compositions, such as the sounds of bells, weaponry, and animals. When selecting a track to superimpose on your video, you have further editing options for that track, including the ability to duplicate it, split it, or alter its loudness.

Extract audio from an existing video

With the use of the InShot app, you also have the option of removing the audio track from the video that you are currently editing. You will be able to alter the audio independently from the video with this. You have the option of modifying its length and volume, as well as duplicating and splitting it. To achieve this, navigate to the Music tool and then tap on the video clip that is located at the very bottom of the screen.

- To extract the audio, select the **Extract option**. You will then be brought to the Music screen, where you will find a distinct audio layer. To make changes, select an **option from the menu at the top**.

Removing background noise from your videos

To get rid of any audio that may already be present in your movie, go to the Volume tool in the toolbar and turn down the volume till it is as low as possible. To erase the audio from all clips, tap the icon that looks like a double checkmark. Altering the volume or disabling the Music tool entirely is options available to you while using this feature.

Add text and stickers

Texts and stickers are two more types of materials that can be used to increase the impact of your videos. The text effects provide you access to a respectable variety of fonts, giving you plenty of options to pick from. You have the option of modifying the font's color as well as its position. Altering the opacity of the text, creating a border around the text, or putting a shadow on the text are some other text customization possibilities. There is a wide variety of content available in the form of animated stickers, emoticons, and GIFs that can be used in your video. There are also speech bubbles, labels, and motivational quotations among the different types of stickers. You may also choose to include a social networking icon, although this will depend on the account you use to post them. It's possible that you can get some of these stickers for free, but others can only be obtained by paying for them. To purchase additional stickers, select the shopping bag icon from the menu.

Add filters and effects

If you'd like to make your videos look more appealing, you have a wide variety of filters from which to pick. Three additional editing categories may be found under the "Filter" heading. These categories are Effect, Filter, and Adjust. Several kinds of glitches, beats, and video styles can produce a wide variety of effects. The stylization effects could be a blur, mosaic, comic, or tilt-shift, depending on your preference. You also can "Distort" a video, which allows you to rotate it in any direction, mirror it, swirl it, fisheye it, or apply a wave effect to it. Sparkly effects are added to your video when you use the "Celebrate" effect. There are many different options available, such as snow, stars, fireworks, ribbons, bubbles, and so on.

You can select the type of lighting that you want to superimpose on top of your video by using the Filter option. There is a wide range of color selections available, from light and natural to darker tones. You can view the other available options by scrolling back and forth. There are a few of them that are free, but there are also in-app purchases that can be made. Last but not least, selecting the Adjust option brings up all of the standard video editing options. It is in this section that you will be able to adjust the luminance, contrast, saturation, and warmth of your video. If you scroll to the side, you will find the remaining editing options, which may include shadows, highlights, curves, and others.

Add a transition

To access the Transition screen, on the video timeline,

- Touch the **clock symbol** that is located between the individual video clips. Choose the transition effect that you want to use.

Add multiple videos in one frame

You may create something resembling a video collage by using the PIP tool to play numerous clips within the same single frame. Use the PIP tool to add the clips you want to layer, and then tap on the tool.

Cut, trim, and split video

Several lengthy videos can be imported and then chopped down to create shorter ones. Some editors simply wish to extract a small or medium section from an existing video and incorporate it into an even larger video they have been working on. Cutting up many videos is the most effective strategy to use when trying to make the beginnings and endings of each video coincide with one another. In addition to cutting down the overall length of the movie, you can also make sure that you obtain the most compelling portion of each shot.

- Choose **the Trim option** or the scissors icon.
- Modify **the sliders** to choose the shot you would like to focus on.
- Touch **the checkmark on the right side** of the screen to complete it.

Splitting a video is yet another method for modifying the length of a video, in addition to trimming and chopping it. With the help of this tool, users can divide a single video into two separate, shorter video snippets. The segment of the video that you wish to split is indicated by the white bar with the red dots on it.

- Choose a video you would like to split. **Touch Trim > Choose Split**.
- Drag **the red-dotted white bar both back and forth** to the exact location where you would like to **split your clip**.
- Touch the **checkmark when you are done**.

Flip, Rotate, Speed

As was to be expected, you may use these tools to rotate the video, flip it, increase or decrease the pace of the video, or any combination of the three. A helpful hint is to break the chunk of the video that you want to slow down and then modify the speed of each segment.

Freeze

With the Freeze tool, you can freeze a frame for the amount of time that you specify. The selected frame will serve as the primary focal point of the video. When maintaining the pointer's position on the frame you wish to freeze, select the Freeze tool from the toolbar.

Removing watermark from videos

If you are editing a video and notice the InShot watermark, simply press on it and watch the promotional video to get rid of it without having to upgrade to the pro version.

Save Video

Using Inshot to create a video is a painless and uncomplicated process. Installing the mobile app is the first step in creating an account.

- After that, you'll need to go to the main menu and tap **"New Video,"** then follow the directions that appear on the screen.

Decide as to what kind of video you would like to produce: a video tutorial, a video journal, or a video story. After you have finished filming and editing the video, you can save it to your phone by

- Tapping the **"Save" button**. To see and share your video, you must first launch the app and then click the **"Video" option**.

Activity

1. Edit your videos with the use of the Inshot app.

CHAPTER 18

SAMSUNG NOTES AND ADVANCED FEATURES

Samsung Notes

You can take notes by writing by hand, using a keyboard, or drawing on the screen. Images and audio files can also be added to your notes.

Creating notes

- Launch the Notes application, select the pen icon, and compose a message. Tapping **the keyboard icon will switch the input method.**
- Once the note is complete, save it by tapping the **Back button.** Select **More options** > Save as file to save the note in a different file format.

If you need to delete any note, all you have to do is tap **Delete.**

Syncing notes

All of your devices that are connected to the same Samsung account allow you to view and modify your notes. To enable sync with Samsung Cloud, launch the **Notes app, select Options > Settings, and then tap the Sync with Samsung Cloud switch.**

Using Note Assist features

Notes can be automatically formatted, summarized, have spelling mistakes fixed, or translated. Once you've created a note, tap the assist feature icon and choose your preferred option.

Composing notes with handwriting

To write or draw in your handwriting, tap the **handwriting icon on the note composer screen.** By extending two fingers across the screen, you can enlarge your handwriting to fit on the screen.

Using favorite pens

Pens that are often used can be saved as favorites and changed by tapping the S Pen button.

- Change the pen's settings, like its type or color, and tap **Done to register your preferred pens.**

To switch the pen, click the **S Pen button** on the note composer screen. You can switch to the preferred pen by repeatedly pressing the S Pen button if you have registered more than one pen.

- The eraser will start to function if you press the S Pen button near the screen; instead, press it while holding it a little bit away.
- To enable this feature if it's off, go to Settings, select **Advanced features > S Pen, and then click the Air actions switch.**

Using the eraser

To remove handwriting from a note, tap and choose the desired area to be erased. As an alternative, pick a region and hold down the S Pen button. Press again to select a different type of eraser.

- **Stroke eraser**: Using a stroke eraser, delete the chosen line.
- **Area eraser:** Use the area eraser to erase just the selected area. By dragging the size adjustment bar, you can change the eraser's size.

You might still be unable to completely erase the targeted area, even with a smaller eraser.

Aligning handwriting or converting to text

- Press the **handwriting icon > Align handwriting** to make your handwriting or drawings straighter horizontally.
- Select the **handwriting icon > Convert to text t**o have the converted text replace your handwriting. Tap Add to when the preview screen shows up.

Recording voice-to-notes

Record your voice as you is writing a note; the content will synchronize with the recording after that. To create a note, tap the **add icon > Voice recording** on the note composer screen. To play the recording, select **a note from the list and tap the play recording icon**. After that, both the recording and the content you produced while it was recording will be shown on the screen.

Clipping content

A note can have content added to it, like an image or a link to a webpage.

- Open the Notes app in a split screen or pop-up view when you're using the Samsung Internet, Messages, or Gallery app and there's something you want to clip.

As an alternative, open the **Air command panel and select Create note, or double tap the screen while holding down the S Pen button.** The note composer screen will have options at the bottom that you can use.

- Choose an option you would like to make use of.

Advanced Features (Tips & Tricks)

Options; on the settings screen, choose advanced features.

- **Advanced intelligence**: Make use of AI functions to facilitate device usage.
- **Bixby:** An easier way to use your device is with Bixby's user interface.
- Smart suggestions: Program the device to identify important details from the chosen text or message, like dates and addresses, and recommend adding them to the calendar or using relevant apps. Based on your past usage of the app, you can also receive recommendations for helpful actions or text to enter.
- **Labs:** Make use of the device's new features.
- **S Pen**: Modify the S Pen's operating parameters.
- **Side button**: Use the Side button to select and launch an application or feature.
- **Multi-window:** Configure the Multi window launch method. Additionally, you can adjust the Multi Window settings.
- **Motions and gestures**: Adjust the parameters and activate the motion feature.
- **One-handed mode**: To make using the device with one hand more convenient, switch on the one-handed operation mode.
- **Screenshots and screen recordings:** Modify the screen recorder and screenshot settings.
- **When sharing content, display contacts**: To share content directly, configure the device to show the contacts you made on the sharing options panel.

Advanced intelligence

Utilize AI features to make your device easier to use. Select **Advanced Features > Advanced Intelligence from the Settings screen.**

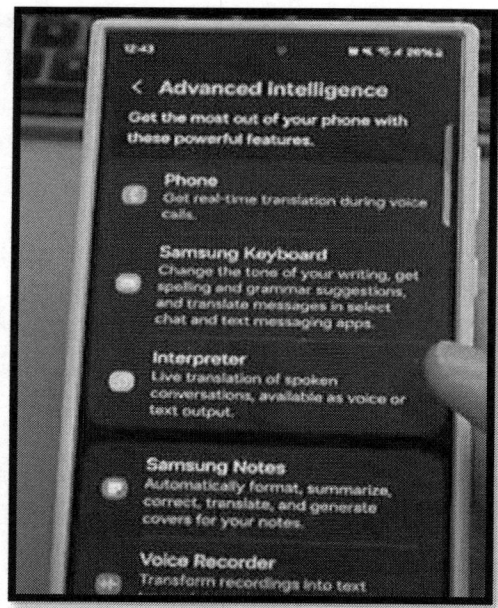

- **Phone**: During voice calls, get translation in real-time.
- **Photo Editor:** Modify photos by cropping, resizing, or moving individuals or objects, and then create a new background to cover any gaps.
- **Samsung Internet**: Access comprehensive translations in addition to concise summaries of webpage content.
- **Samsung Keyboard**: Modify writing style, receive grammar and spelling advice, and translate text messages in a few chosen chat and text messaging apps.
- **Samsung Notes**: Enhance notes by automatically creating covers for them, summarizing, formatting, and editing them.
- **Voice Recorder**: Convert audio files into text summaries and transcripts for editing or translating.
- **Interpreter:** Real-time translation of spoken dialogue into text or speech output.

Motions and gestures

Activate the motion feature and adjust the parameters.

- Select **Advanced Features > Motions and Gestures from the Settings screen.**
- **Lift to wake**: Configure the gadget so that when you pick it up, the screen will turn on.
- **Double tap to turn the screen on** Double tapping anywhere on the screen while it is off will turn on the screen. This is how you set up your device to turn on the screen.

- **Double tap to turn the screen off**: Double tapping space on the Home screen or the locked screen will cause the screen to turn off on the device.
- **Alert when phone picked up**: Configure the gadget to notify you upon picking it up if there are any new messages or missed calls.
- **Mute with gestures**: You can use motions or gestures to mute specific sounds on the device.
- **Palm swipe to capture**: Swipe your palm left or right across the screen to take a screenshot: Configure the device to take a screenshot when you do this. The captured photos are available to view in the Gallery. Some apps and features prevent you from taking screenshots while you're using them.

Video call effects

Among the features you can use is the ability to alter the background during video calls. Open the notification panel on the screen of the video calling app, swipe down, and select **Video Call Effects**.

- **Background**: During video calls, adjust or blur the background.
- **Face**: Give your face some cosmetic effects.
- **Color tone**: Modify the brightness and color tone of the screen.
- **Auto framing**: Activate or deactivate this feature. When you activate this feature, the camera automatically adjusts the zoom and shooting angle by identifying and following the people in your video calls.

Dual Messenger

Use two different accounts for the same messenger app after installing the second app.

- Select **Advanced Features**

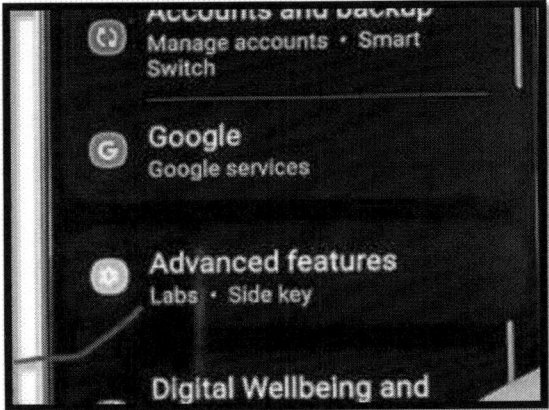

> **Dual Messenger**

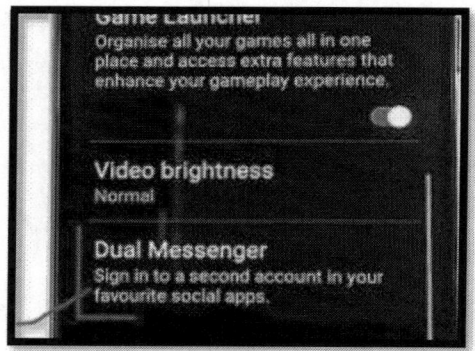

- **From the Settings screen**. Apps with support will show up.
- To install the second app, tap **the app's switch.** You're going to install the second app. The icon for the second app will appear.
  - Depending on the app, the Dual Messenger feature might not be accessible.
  - The app's functionality might be restricted for the second app.

To uninstall a second application, follow the settings below;

- Select **Advanced Features > Dual Messenger from the Settings screen.**
- To uninstall an app, tap **its switch and select Uninstall**. The second app's associated data will be completely erased.

Bixby

An easier way to use your device is with Bixby's user interface. You can type text or converse with Bixby. When you ask Bixby to launch a feature or display information, Bixby will comply. Go to www.samsung.com/bixby for additional details. Bixby is limited to a few languages and might not be accessible in some areas.

Starting Bixby

To open Bixby, press and hold the Side button. It will show the Bixby intro page. The Bixby screen will show up after you choose the language to use with Bixby, log into your Samsung account, and finish the setup by following the on-screen directions.

Using Bixby

Tell Bixby what you want while holding down the Side button. As an alternative, state your desires while saying the wake-up phrase. Say "How's the weather today?" while holding down the Side button, for instance. The screen will display the weather information. During a conversation, you can carry on speaking with Bixby without tapping or pressing the Side button if it asks you a question.

- To enable Bixby if you can't find its icon on the Apps screen, go to Settings, select **Advanced features >Bixby, and then click the Show Bixby on the Apps screen switch.**

Waking up Bixby using your voice

Bixby can be spoken to by saying "Hello, Bixby" or "Bixby". To get Bixby to respond to your voice, register your voice.

- In the Bixby app, select **Settings > Voice wake-up after opening.**
- To turn it on, just **tap the switch.**
- Under the **Wake-up phrase, choose the wake-up phrase you prefer.**
- To activate it, tap the Respond to my voice switch.
- To finish the setup, adhere to the instructions displayed on the screen.
  Saying the wake-up phrase and striking up a conversation is now possible.

Bixby Vision

A service called Bixby Vision offers many features that rely on image recognition. By identifying objects, Bixby Vision can be used to conduct informational searches. Make use of all the helpful Bixby Vision features.

- The size, format, and resolution of the image may affect this feature's availability or the accuracy of the search results.
- Regarding the product information that Bixby Vision provides, Samsung is not liable.

Opening Bixby Vision

Open Bixby Vision by utilizing any of these techniques.

- Select **BIXBY VISION from the list of shooting modes in the Camera app by tapping MORE.**
- Choose an image in the Gallery app, and then tap **the eye icon.**
- Touch and hold an image in the Samsung Internet app, then select **Search with Bixby Vision.**
- Launch the **Bixby Vision app** if you have added the app's icon to the Apps screen.

Using Bixby Vision

- Start the **Bixby Vision app.**
- Choose a feature to utilize.

- **TRANSLATE:** Identify and translate text from pictures or documents.
- **TEXT:** Extract and identify text from documents or images.
- **DISCOVER:** Look up related information and pictures online that resemble the recognized object.

Using the S Pen

Below are necessary cautions that must be observed when making use of the S pen;

- The S Pen should not be bent or used with excessive pressure when in use. There could be damage to the S Pen or deformity to the nib.
- Avoid applying force to the screen while using the S Pen. Pen nib deformation is possible.
- Certain actions with the S Pen, like charging or tapping the screen, might not function if there is a magnet close by.
- You can use other S Pen features, like tapping the screen or the Air command features, even if the S Pen is completely depleted.
- The device might not recognize S Pen actions if you use it at sharp angles on the screen.
- Before using the S Pen, empty the slot of any water that may have gotten inside.
- Take the S Pen to an authorized service center or a Samsung service center if it isn't functioning properly.

Detaching the S Pen

To detach the S Pen, press its end. After that, take the S Pen out of the slot. Replace the S Pen in the slot and press until it clicks into place to store it.

- To configure a task to be executed upon detaching the S Pen, navigate to **Settings, select Advanced features**

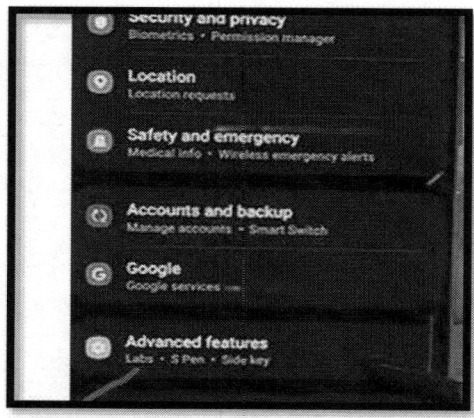

> S Pen

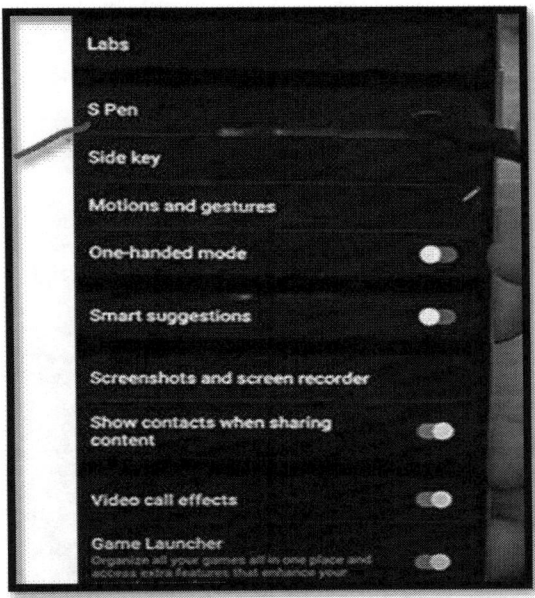

When S Pen is removed, and then picks an appropriate option.

How to Charge the S Pen

Before you can use the S Pen button to remotely control apps, the S Pen needs to be charged. The S Pen will begin to charge as soon as you place it in the slot. The S Pen will only charge when the device is charging if the Air action feature is disabled.

Allow multiple S Pens

- Select **Advanced features > S Pen > More S Pen settings after opening Settings.** To activate it, tap the **Allow multiple S Pens switch**.

Air actions (Controlling apps remotely with the S Pen)

Using the S Pen that is Bluetooth Low Energy (BLE) connected to your device, you can control apps remotely. For instance, holding down the S Pen button allows you to launch apps like the camera app. additionally; you can snap a picture with the camera app by simply **tapping the button once.** When listening to music, you can adjust the volume by raising the **S Pen while holding down the S Pen button and lowering it to decrease the volume.**

- You can't use the Air actions feature until the S Pen is charged.
- The icon will show up on the status bar as soon as you remove the S Pen from its

slot. The S Pen will be disconnected from the device and the icon will turn gray if it is empty, too far away from the device, has obstructions or external interference between it and the device, or all of these situations. Re-inserting the S Pen into the slot will re-establish the device-S Pen connection and enable the Air actions feature.

Taking pictures with the S Pen

You can snap pictures without setting a timer by simply pressing the S Pen button, even when your device is placed at a distance. To enable the feature, navigate to **Advanced features > S Pen > Air actions in Settings,**

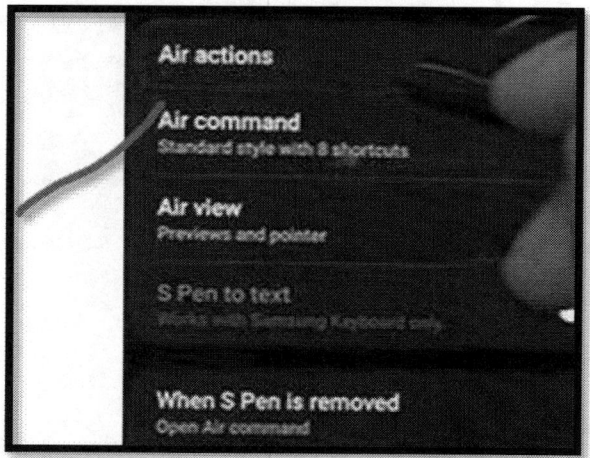

Tap it, and then press the switch.

- Get the Camera app open.
- To take a picture, press **the S Pen button once.**
- Press and hold the **S Pen button to snap a sequence of images.**
- Move the S Pen left or right while holding down **the S Pen button to switch the shooting mode.**
- Double-clicking the **S Pen button will switch between cameras.**

Resetting your S Pen

Reset the S Pen and reconnect it if there are frequent connection issues or disconnections.

- Put the S Pen in the designated slot. Next, select A**dvanced features > S Pen > More options > S Pen reset from the Settings menu.**
  - Only S Pens that have been approved by Samsung and support Bluetooth Low Energy (BLE) can be connected.

- When the S Pen is connected to the device, do not remove it. This will cause the process to stop.

Air Command (Launching S Pen features and apps directly)

Direct access to frequently used apps and S Pen features is available through the Air Command menu. Using the S Pen, tap the **Air command icon to bring up the Air command panel where you can choose the desired function or app.** Hovering the S Pen over the Air command icon in apps that support the Air actions feature allows you to see which actions are available in each app. Drag the Air command icon to a new location to reposition it. Drag the icon to the **Remove button** at the bottom of the screen to get rid of it.

- Open Settings, select **Advanced features > S Pen > Air command, and then tap the Show Air command icon** switch to enable it if the Air command icon is not visible on the screen. Hovering the **S Pen over the screen and pressing the S Pen button will open the Air command panel** if you have enabled the Open Air command with the Pen button switch.
- **Make a note**: Open a pop-up window and make notes. Alternatively, you can double-tap the screen while holding down the S Pen button to activate this feature.
- **See every note:** Use the Samsung Notes app to view all of your notes.
- **Smart select**: Choose an area with the S Pen and carry out operations, like sharing or saving.
- **Screen write:** Take screenshots and crop a portion of the image to write or draw on them. An extended page, like a webpage, can also have its hidden content as well as its current content captured.
- **Magnify:** To make a portion of the screen larger, move the S Pen over it.
- **PENUP:** Share your artwork, view the creations of others, and receive helpful drawing advice.
- **Write on the calendar:** To write or draw on the calendar, open the Calendar app and select the desired date.
- **Add**: Customize the Air command panel with shortcuts to commonly used applications.

Smart Select

To perform actions, like sharing or saving, select an area with the S Pen. Additionally, you can make a GIF out of a portion of a video by selecting it.

- Open the Air command panel, select **Smart Select,** and **select the content you want to capture, such as a portion of an image.**
- To select content, select a desired shape icon from the toolbar and drag the **S Pen across it.**
- To utilize the S Pen with the selected area, choose an option.
    - **Pin**: Attach the chosen region to the display. The image can also be inserted into other applications, like Samsung Notes. To view the image in the other app, drag it there.
    - **Copy:** Copy and paste the chosen portion into a different app or onto a different device that is connected to your Samsung account.
    - **Extract**: Take text out of the chosen region.
    - **Write**: In the designated area, write or draw.
    - **Share:** Give others access to the chosen area.
    - **Save**: Save the chosen region in the Gallery.

Capturing an area from a video

Choose a region and record it as a GIF while the video is playing.

- Open the Air command panel and select **Smart Select** whenever you see something you want to record while watching a video.
- Press **GIF on the toolbar.**
- Modify the capturing area's size and location.
- To begin recording, tap **Record.**
    - Make sure the video is playing before you record it.
    - The screen will show you the maximum amount of time you can record a section of the video.
    - The sound of an area captured from a video will not be recorded.
- Press **Stop** to end the recording.

Screen write

Take screenshots so you can annotate, sketch, or crop a portion of the image.

- Open the Air command panel, selects **Screen Write, and selects the content you wish to record.**
  The editing toolbar appears and an automatic capture of the current screen is made.
- Take down a note on the screen grab.
- Get the screenshot saved or shared. You can also always check the Gallery for screenshots.

Translate

To translate a text, move the S Pen pointer over it. Additionally, the text's units will be converted.

- Open the **Air command panel**, selects **Translate, and then selects the text you wish to translate.**
- On the translator panel at the top of the screen, choose the **languages you want to use.**
  By tapping the **T icon,** you can switch the text between words and sentences.
- To translate or convert a text or unit, just hover the S Pen over it. It will show the translated text. Tap the speaker icon to hear how the original text is pronounced. The language you choose may prevent the icon from appearing.

Write on the calendar

Write or draw your schedule on the calendar screen to complete it.

- Navigate to the **Air command panel, select Write on Calendar, and then enter your schedule there. Once you're done, select Save.** To make changes, simply tap the pencil icon.

S Pen to text

Anything you write with the S Pen can be programmed on the device to be converted to text.

- To activate S Pen to text, open **Settings, select Advanced features > S Pen > S Pen to text, and then tap the switch**.
  Tap How to edit to see how to edit text with the S Pen.
- Use the S Pen to write in a text input field, like a search field or address bar. Text will be generated from the handwriting.

Air view

To view a pop-up window with information or preview content, move the S Pen over the item on the screen. Action buttons may show up in the preview window of certain apps.

- To enable this feature if it's off, go to **Settings, select Advanced features > S Pen, and then click the Air view switch.**

Pen Select (Selecting items quickly with the S Pen)

- To select multiple items or text, drag the **S Pen over lists of items or text while**

holding down the S Pen button. The chosen objects or text can also be shared with others or copied and pasted into another app.

Screen-off memos

Memos can be written on the screen without turning it on. Remove the S Pen when the screen is off, or double tap the screen while holding down the S Pen button.

- After writing a memo, it will be saved to Samsung Notes when you tap S**ave or put the S Pen back into the slot.**

Pinning a memo on the Always on Display

Tap the pin icon on the Always on Display to pin a screen off memo. There is still time to save the pinned memo.

- Double-tap **the pen icon to make changes to the pinned memo.** The original memo will be saved to Samsung Notes if you pin the edited memo to the **Always on Display once more. Double-tapping the double arrow will minimize the pinned memo.**

Unlocking the screen using the S Pen

By pressing the S Pen button, you can unlock a locked screen while the S Pen is connected.

- Select **Advanced features > S Pen > More S Pen settings after opening Settings**.
- To activate the S Pen, simply tap **the unlock switch**. You can now use the S Pen button to unlock the screen.
  - Only when the screen lock method is configured is the S Pen unlock feature available.
  - The S Pen needs to be plugged into your device to use this feature.

Tips, tricks, and maps to enjoy the most from your Galaxy S24 series

Customize the side key

By default, when the side key is pressed down, it activates Bixby which is the amazing virtual assistant that has been provided with this device. If you happen to be a fan of virtual assistants you will surely find this feature amazing. Nonetheless, most people still prefer the old-fashioned power-off menu when they touch and hold the side key. Fortunately, you can easily change the side-key operation on your Galaxy S24 handset.

- Simply open the **Settings app** from the **App Drawer**, or slide down the notification tray and touch **the gear icon**.
- Scroll down and touch **Advanced features > Side key**.

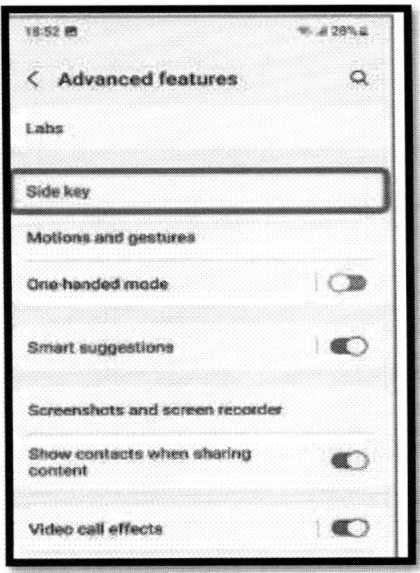

- Once you are in, you then personalize the press-and-hold feature so you can use it to either open the power menu or wake Bixby.

Personalize Accent Colors

Out of the box, the Samsung Galaxy S24 utilizes OneUI, which is based on Android 13. In a similar vein, you also get to try out the new and improved Material Design by Google. You create a design ethos that is bursting at the seams with options for personalization. The ability to change the Samsung Galaxy S24's accent colors is one of its greatest features. For instance, your wallpaper may propose a color scheme that can be used as the basis for a system-wide theme. Colors from the palette will be used throughout the user interface, icons, and Samsung's preinstalled software.

- To get this done; **tap and hold on a space on your home screen**. In the options displayed, touch **Wallpaper and style**.
- Touch the **Color palette** then enable the **toggle close to the Color palette**.

Enable dark mode

The displays on the Samsung Galaxy S24 series are among the greatest you'll find on a smartphone. The phones' AMOLED displays also make it a good idea to make use of the Dark Mode. In addition to satisfying a personal taste, switching to dark mode on an

AMOLED display has been shown to conserve more power. Therefore, learning how to allow and schedule the dark mode on your Samsung Galaxy S24 is one of the best tricks for this device.

- To have the dark mode enabled, **swipe down the notification tray to open the Quick settings page**. Swipe to the left of the screen to show the second page then **touch Dark Mode**.

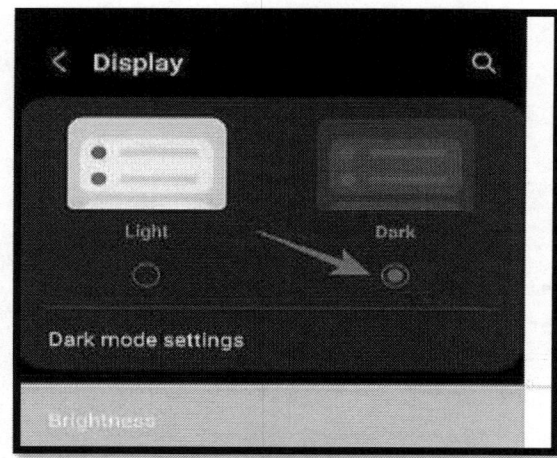

- Note that you can also choose to schedule the dark mode if you wish. Simply touch **the Dark mode settings** then enable the **toggle close to Turn on as scheduled**.

Add Smart Widgets

The creation of Smart Widgets is another amazing feature of the S24 series. These widgets can be stacked and can also be personalized.

- To add Smart Widgets to your home screen, **touch and hold a space on your screen > touch Widgets**.

Enable Dolby Atmos

The dual speakers of the Samsung Galaxy S24 have been fine-tuned by audio industry titans AKG. Dolby Atmos audio support is included, too. This function is, alas, turned off by default. Yet, the following workaround makes it simple to activate Dolby Atmos on your Samsung S24 smartphone.

- Touch **Settings > Sounds and vibration > Sound quality and effects. Enable the toggle close to Dolby Atmos and Dolby Atmos for gaming**.

Get notifications previews in Air View

Move the S-Pen over an object on the screen to open a pop-up window containing additional information or to view a preview of the content. On the preview screen of certain applications, you will find buttons labeled **"Action."**

- If this feature is switched off, open **Settings**, touch **Advanced features > S Pen**, and then touch the **Air view toggle to have it turned on**.

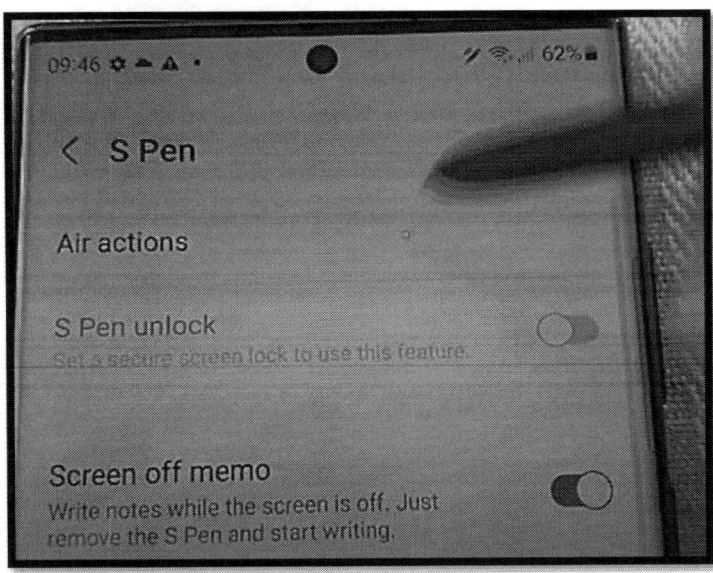

When you want to pick several items or text, press and hold the button on the S Pen, and then drag the tip of the S Pen over text or item lists. You also have the option to copy and paste the items or text that you have picked into another application or start sharing them with other people.

Use handwriting with Gboard

The Gboard app already includes support for handwritten input, and it works well with the S Pen. **Even pressure sensitivity can be supported by it. The setup is quick and simple:**

- Open the **Gboard settings** by touching the arrow at the top of the keyboard then touch the cog icon.

- Open the **menu for languages**.

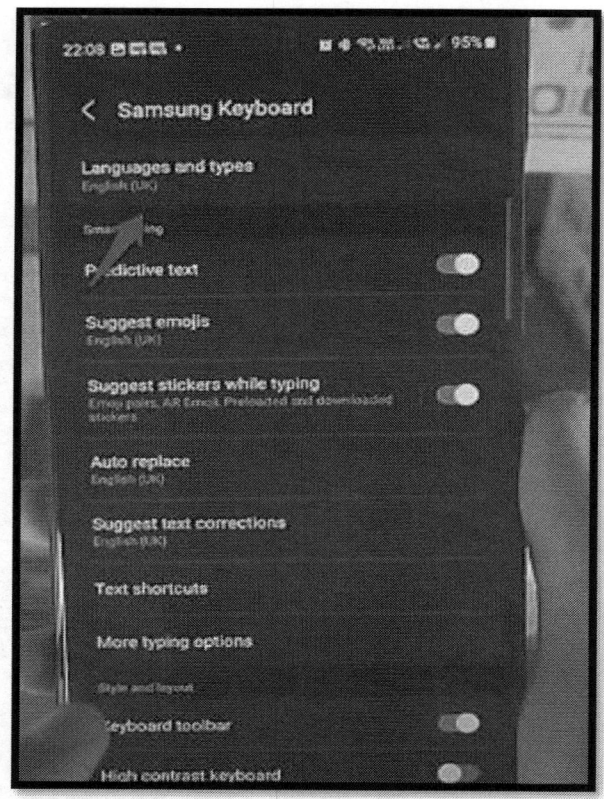

- Touch **Add keyboard**.
- Touch your preferred language and pick **Handwriting** from the layouts listed.
- Touch **Done**.

You'll notice that the key that used to be for emoji has been replaced by an icon of a globe on your keyboard. You may still access all of your emoticons by holding down the button for an extended period. Just touching the globe will toggle between the QWERTY keyboard and the handwriting input method. Even when presented with illegible glyphs, handwriting is a quick and accurate method of communication. If you are using Samsung's keyboard, the layout will automatically transition to handwriting mode when the S Pen is detected. But, I find that Samsung's keyboard is inferior in virtually every way to what Gboard has to offer, so it's recommended to switch instead.

Quickly markup text with the S Pen

The process of copying and pasting text can be a chore, particularly if you are trying to highlight the precise text that you want to emphasize. The S-Pen comes into its own in this situation. Press and hold down the button located on the side of the stylus, and then drag it across the text that you want to copy. There is no need to hold down the button for an extended time to bring up the appropriate menu; everything works swiftly and accurately.

Gesture lock with S Pen

To activate Android's gesture navigation, you can swipe up from the bottom or sides of the screen while using the S Pen. While that is acceptable for ordinary use, it may become a pain when you are trying to write or draw something. It is quite frustrating when you need to write to the border of the screen, but by accident, you trigger the back gesture, which causes all of your work to be erased. To your great relief, there is a simple solution.

- Open **Settings** then open the **Display menu**.
- Scroll **downward**s and open the **Navigation Bar menu**.
- Scroll down and Switch on **Block gestures with S Pen**.

Customize screenshots with Air Command

When capturing a screenshot, it's rather uncommon to wish to capture an image in its entirety but just only a portion of it. You would normally have to open up your gallery and trim the screenshot after the fact; however, the S Pen can help you save time doing both of these things.

To access Air Command,

- Click the **S Pen button** while the device is hovering above the screen and then select **Smart Select** from the menu that appears. After that, simply move the **S Pen** over the subject you want to obtain, and you're done.

Yet, Smart Select is capable of far more than simply grabbing square images off your screen. In addition, there is a lasso tool, which can snap round screenshots, and a GIF capture option, which is our particular favorite of these features. After selecting this option, move the box over the portion of the screen that you want to record, select the quality of the GIF, and then press the record button. This one will come in handy quite a bit for those of you who enjoy creating memes and animated GIFs. Even though there are tons of other things you can do with the S Pen, such as controlling media and the camera app with air movements, these are the ones that you will find to be the most helpful. In addition to the features that are already incorporated into the system, users also have access to a variety of apps that may be used with the S pen.

Pencil on Samsung Calendar events

Preference has always been for Samsung's Calendar software rather than Google Calendar, and one of the reasons for this preference is the ability to scribble on the app using the S Pen. Although scheduling events and reminders is a simpler and more effective method for ensuring that you remember something, painting is a more enjoyable way to accomplish the same goal. By highlighting and circling important dates, you may make them easier to find from the monthly view. As a wonderful added benefit, you can even recreate your favorite memes using this feature.

Write, draw, and annotate with Samsung notes

On the screen of the note composer, touch the convert handwriting to text icon to either draw or write in your unique handwriting. You can choose to insert your handwriting in a much larger size if you enlarge the screen by spreading two of your fingers on it.

Editing handwritten notes

Edit handwritten notes with the use of various editing options like cutting, resizing, or **moving.**

- When there is handwriting on the note, touch the s**elect and edit icon**. If you would like to change the shape of the selection touch the **select and edit icon again**.
- Touch or draw **a line** around the input to choose. If you would like to drag the input to a different location, choose the input option then move it to another location. To modify the size of the selection, touch **the input** and move a corner of the frame that is displayed.
- Modify **the input** with the use of the options available.

Straightening content horizontally

You can have your handwriting and drawings straightened horizontally;

- Write or draw on the screen and touch the **Straighten icon**.

Changing styles

The style of your handwriting and drawings can be modified. All you have to do is write or draw on the screen, touch an alphabet twice, and choose a specific color or line thickness you prefer. Once done, direct the S Pen where you would like the style applied. When the forward pointing arrow is displayed, touch the exact place you would like to modify the style.

Relax with an S Pen and Samsung PENUP

The Samsung PENUP app is a sketching and coloring program that is pre-installed on the S24 Ultra. Even though it only has a few features, the app is nonetheless enjoyable to play around with because of its intuitive interface. This app is not the right choice for you if you want to utilize the S Pen to produce genuine works of art. On the other hand, if you want to doodle, the app provides everything you could need. The coloring mode in PENUP is where it shines. There are hundreds of different pictures available for selection, and more are being added daily. It is a fantastic idea to offer your child the S Pen and encourage them to be creative if you want to keep them occupied for a short time.

Use Pentastic to tweak your Air Commands

Good Lock is a collection of apps that, when used together, provide you the ability to personalize practically every aspect of your Galaxy smartphone, including the S Pen. You have your choice to make between five different variations of Air Command, each of which was drawn from a different iteration of the Galaxy Note. After you have selected the style that you prefer, you may modify the degree of dimming and blurring, and you can even select an image to use as the background. There are seven different pointers available for use with the S Pen, ranging from the more conventional arrows to endearing animal stickers. You can alter the size of each of the pointer styles, as well as import PNG pictures to create your very own. In addition, you have the option of picking from one of seven different sets of sound effects that will be played whenever the stylus is taken from and reinserted into the phone. If you'd rather, you can also add your effects if you'd like. Last but not least, Pentastic includes a double-tap shortcut that is activated when the S Pen button is held down and double taps are performed on the screen. This allows you to designate several different S Pen capabilities to it, like the ability to write on your calendar, magnify the screen, and activate Smart Select. You may also designate the shortcut to whatever program you choose, and then use the double-tap gesture to start it. If none of those options appeal to you, there is another alternative.

Create images quickly using the S Pen with Infinite Painter

Infinite Painter is one of the best drawing apps available for Android devices, and it is also the app that most closely resembles Apple's Procreate for iPad. There is a wide selection of brushes and tools available, and each one may be customized to meet one's specific needs. The S Pen is supported in every way, including its pressure sensitivity and the mapping of its side buttons; however, to make the latter feature operational, you will need to put in some effort. You have the option of assigning the S Pen button to control the eyedropper, undo/redo, the blend mode, and undo/redo operations. The configuration of that is straightforward, but there is a catch: pressing the button will still call up Air Command. You will need to come up with a Bixby Routine to get past this obstacle.

- Open the **Bixby Routines app**.
- Touch **Add Routine** on the lower part of the bar.

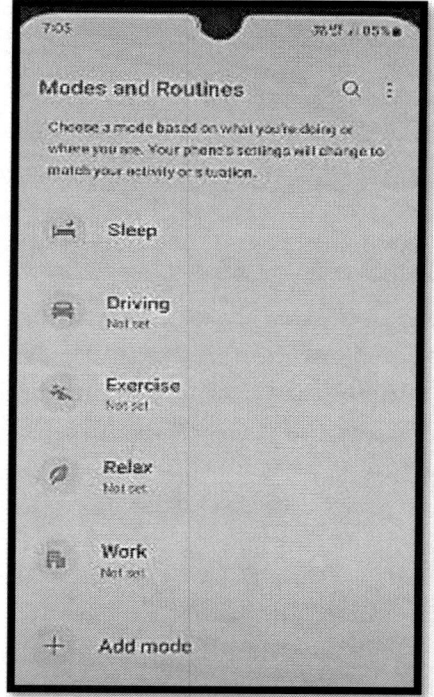

- Touch the Plus icon beneath the If subheading.
- Touch App opened and then located the Painter in the list of applications.
- Touch the Plus sign beneath the then subheading.
- Find and open Air Command with the Pen button and touch Off.
- Touch Next, give your routine a name, and touch Done.

As soon as that is done, the Air Command button will no longer be active while you are using the Infinite Painter app, and you will be able to utilize the S Pen button for any other function within the application that you like.

Fill out documents with Adobe Fill & Sign

The Samsung Notes is a capable device to use even if signing legal documents is something you only do on an infrequent basis. If, on the other hand, your work involves a lot of contracts and other documents that need to be signed and initialized, then using Adobe Fill & Sign will be a huge time saver for you. Your signature and initials only need to be written down once, and after that, the application will let you place a copy of them wherever it is required. This may be accomplished with ease with the S Pen, both in terms of generating your signature and placing it on the page. The application also enables you to fill in checkboxes and add text fields that require typing. Even while you could do all of this with your finger, using the S Pen will make it much simpler to get everything lined up exactly how you want it.

My Files App

The files stored in this device can be accessed and also managed with so much ease.

- Open the **My Files app**.
- To check for data that is not necessary and also ensure the storage of the device is freed up, touch **Analyze storage**.
- If you would like to locate files or folders, touch the search icon which looks like the eye shape.

Activity

1. Utilize AI features to make life easier.
2. Add effects to your video calls.
3. Make use of two different accounts for the same messenger.
4. Make use of Bixby for ease of navigation.
5. Take pictures with the S pen.
6. Control apps remotely with the S pen.
7. Capture an area from a video.
8. Use handwriting with Gboard
9. Write, draw, and annotate with Samsung notes.

CHAPTER 19

SAMSUNG HEALTH

Samsung Health is an application that helps users maintain a healthy lifestyle by facilitating regular exercise. The app, which can be downloaded on both Android and iOS devices, monitors your health by recording data from your daily activities. This software is also the standard for Samsung's line of wearable health and fitness trackers. Samsung's Health app fills in the blanks. The fitness app has a plethora of features, including goal setting, stat viewing, step tracking, and more. Additionally, it is available in a wide range of display sizes, from your wristwatch to your smartphone to your smart TV. The Samsung Health app keeps track of a lot of the fundamentals. It is an excellent resource for keeping track of your health as a whole, and it acts as a catchall for the most vital information about its users. Workouts, steps, active minutes, heart rate, and sleep may all be recorded.

Both automatic and manual sleep tracking are available in Samsung Health, depending on the device you use. SpO2 levels, snoring, and noise levels in the environment can all be monitored by fitness trackers and other devices that are compatible with this technology. Smartwatch owners with a Samsung Galaxy Watch 4 or Galaxy Watch 5 can also take advantage of Samsung's Sleep Coaching feature. By syncing your watch with Samsung's Health app, the organization can examine your sleeping habits. Depending on your sleeping patterns, a specific animal will be assigned to you after roughly a week. The app analyzes your data and creates a personalized sleep improvement plan over several weeks. Weight, water consumption, and calorie counts are all measurable with this app. It won't be the most sophisticated calorie counter available, but it can serve as a food journal if that's what you're after. Depending on the model, the Samsung Health app can also monitor blood glucose levels, blood pressure, and blood oxygen levels in addition to the user's heart rate and stress levels. Finally, the app will record information about women's health, such as their cycles and symptoms.

How to Install Samsung Health on a Galaxy Phone

To have Samsung Health installed on your phone you will have to download it from the Google Play Store. Once downloaded, open the application and click **Create account then complete the necessary information. Once you are signed into the application, there are four basic tabs that you can navigate to;**

- **Home**: Under its name, this tab is the base of the Samsung Health app. This is the very place where you can configure and also track your goals. You can touch the Home tab to take a review of your stats or to add data which includes weight, food, water intake, and a lot more manually to the application. Scrolling down this tab reveals the Manage item option which you can use to either include or take away some measurables from your home screen.

- **Together**: You can enter challenges and compare your stats with other Samsung Health users on the tab titled "Together." Your social network can be a great source of motivation for your pals as they pursue their own health goals.
- **Fitness**: Touch the fitness tab and commence a 15-minute workout video, listen to a sleep story, or read about PMS. This tab is home to a lot of libraries that deal with exercise and wellness resources which include workout programs, videos, content from Samsung Health TV partners, and also various tools for women's health.
- **My page**: It is in this section of the Samsung Health app that users can make changes to their profile. Important values like calorie expenditure and heart rate ranges can be calculated with the addition of your gender, height, weight, and date and place of birth. On a scale from one to four, you can choose your normal daily activity level. The "My page" tab shows you more than just your basic profile information; it also displays statistics like your weekly totals, personal records, and badges you've achieved.

Samsung Health, in contrast to competitors like Google Fit and Apple Health, does not allow users to connect to a wide variety of "connected services," as Samsung calls them. Among the notable exceptions are the health and fitness tracking platforms Technogym and the renowned running and cycling app Strava. Samsung smartwatches are among the many health and fitness devices that are compatible with Samsung Health.

- By selecting the **menu (the three stacked lines at the top right of your screen)**, and then selecting **Settings**, you may see a full list of supported gadgets within the app.
- Select **Accessories** from the drop-down menu and then explore the available gadgets.

Activity

1. Install Samsung Health on your device.

CHAPTER 20

MAKE A CALL WITH GOOGLE DUO

Google Duo allows you to make voice or video calls to other users. Every call is processed through either the data plan associated with your mobile device or through a Wi-Fi connection. Calls don't utilize your mobile minutes. If you use the data on your mobile device, you may be subject to additional fees.

Before you start

Wi-Fi and cellular data allow you to stay in face-to-face contact with friends and family at any hour of the day or night. You may use the Google Duo app to make video calls on a Galaxy phone, which is the app that is installed automatically.

Step 1: Install Duo

If you don't have Duo installed already go to the Google Play Store > search for Duo and Tap to have it installed.

Step 2: Check your Phone number

Insert the phone number of the smartphone you want to enroll in your current Duo 2-Factor Authentication account. After entering the phone number, make sure to check the box confirming that the phone number you entered is accurate.

Step 3: Connect your Google account

When you link your Google Account to Duo, the following will occur:

You may utilize Duo throughout different devices. Anyone who has access to your phone number or other information associated with your Google Account, such as your Gmail address, will be able to see that you use the Duo app and can call you using it. When you sign up for Duo, you will be given the option to add your Google Account. Alternatively, you can include it at a later time using the settings menu in the app. When you set up Duo, you are required to include a Google Account so that you may use it on the web.

- Open the already downloaded **Duo app**.
- Touch M**enu > Settings > Google Account**.
- Touch the **Google Account** you would like to add. If you do not have an account on your device touch **Add account**.
- Follow the steps popping up on your screen.

Start a Video or Voice Call

Ensure you have the latest version of the Duo if not you have updated it on the Google Play Store. Once completed, follow the steps below to start either a video or voice call;

- Open the **Google Duo app**.
- At the top of the app, **locate contacts or dial a number you would like to call**.
- Touch **the contact or number you would like to call**.
- Choose your preferred option;
  - To make a video call, touch **the Video icon**.
  - To make an audio call, touch **the green color call icon**.

Use Google Duo on your Google Home device

You can use Google Duo to make calls to any Google Home device, including Smart Displays with Google Assistant, as long as you are signed in to that device.

Note: You need to make sure that the language of your Google Assistant is set to either English from the United States, English from the United Kingdom, Canadian English, or French from Canada.

- On your device, open the **Duo app**.
- At the top of your contact list, touch **Call Home**.

Start a group video call

You can have a group video call on Duo as it can take up to 32 participants in just one group video call. This means you can reach your extended family at once with the use of the group video call.

Create a group

- Open the **Google Duo app**.
- At the lower right corner of the screen, touch **New Call > Create group**.
- Pick **your contacts**.
- Touch **Done**.
- Touch **Start**.

You can give the group a name. Touch the Edit icon, insert a name, and touch Save. The name will be displayed for everyone in the group.

Invite someone to a group call via a link

With just a link, you can add someone to your group call.

Follow the steps below;

- Open the **Duo app**.
- At the lower right corner, touch **New call > Create group**.
- Choose **your preferred contacts**.
- Touch **Done**.
- If you would like to share the link or include more contacts, touch **Copy or Share**.
  - When the link is clicked on a computer, it will take the recipient to the website **duo.google.com**.
  - When the link is tapped on a mobile device, the **Google Duo app launches automatically if the recipient already has it installed**.
  - If the recipient is using a mobile device and does not already have Google Duo installed, the link will launch **Google Duo in either the Google Play or App Store when it is tapped**.
- Touch **Start**.

Phone an existing group or connect to an ongoing group call

With Duo, you can join an ongoing group call with so much ease. Simply follow the settings below to get this done;

- Open the **Google Duo app**.
- At the bottom right corner, touch **New Call**.
- Beneath Groups, call **a group or join a live group**. Be on the lookout, if you happen to see Live under the name of the group this means the call is live and you can join.
  - **To call an existing group**: touch **the group name or participants > Start**.
  - **To join a live group call**: touch **the name of the group or participants > Join**.

How to change the name of the Group, add members, reset group links, or leave a group

When it comes to using group calls, Duo gives you a wide variety of options to choose from. You have the option to modify the name of the group, invite additional people to join the group, reset the link to the group, and eventually, you could decide that you have had enough of being a part of the group and decide to leave.

- Open the **Google Duo app**.
- At the lower right corner, touch **New Call**.
- Beneath Groups, touch **a group > More options**.
- Choose **your preferred option** and follow the instructions displayed on the screen.

Suspicious Group

When you receive a group invites from Google Duo and it contains users who are not in your contacts or who have blocked accounts, Google Duo flags the group as suspicious. Google Duo will not provide you with any information regarding the members of the group that you have blocked. You are free to join the group or to reject doing so. If you join, Google Duo will not automatically unblock anybody that you have previously barred.

Remove members from the group

You also have the option of removing a member of the group on your own. If the individual that you blocked clicks the link that took them to the group in the first place, they will be informed that the group no longer exists. This is an important point to keep in mind. The link to the group gets updated for everyone else who is a part of the group.

- Open the **Google Duo app**.
- At the lower right of the screen, touch **New Call**.
- Beneath **Groups, touch Group**.
- Touch and hold the **contact you would like to remove**.
- Touch **Remove** from group. You can also simply choose to block the group member.

Making Google Duo calls from other applications

You can make Duo calls from different applications. In this section, the various applications from which this can be done will be explored;

Phone app

If you would like to make use of Google Duo with the Phone app;

- Open the **Phone app**.
- Choose your preferred **contact > History**.
- On the lower part of the screen, touch the **Video call icon**.

Contacts app

You can make use of Google Duo with the Contacts app;

- Open the **Contacts app**.
- Launch the **info card of a contact.**
- Touch the **Video icon**.

Messages app

You can make use of Google Duo with the Messages app;

- Open the **Messages app**.
- Start **a conversation**.
- At the top of the screen, **make a video call**.

Google Assistant

You can launch a Google Duo video call when you say or enter;

- OK Google, **Duo calls (insert the name of the person)**
- OK Google, **Video call (Insert the name of the person)**

Activity

1. Install Duo on your phone.
2. Connect your Google account
3. Make calls with the use of Duo.
4. Make Google Duo calls from other applications.

CHAPTER 21

TROUBLESHOOTING TIPS

Do you have any issues with your Samsung Galaxy S24? If so, you're not by yourself, so don't worry. This chapter will teach you how to resolve some of the most frequent issues with the Samsung Galaxy S24 smartphone.

Heating Problem on your Samsung Galaxy S24

Don't panic if your Samsung Galaxy S24 smartphone is experiencing a heating issue. This is a typical issue that can be resolved with a few adjustments.

Solution

- Don't panic if your Samsung Galaxy S24 smartphone is experiencing a heating issue. This is a typical issue that can be resolved with a few adjustments.
- Unplug the phone once it has finished charging. It frequently results in overheating issues.
- Use a thin back cover, please. Wearing a thick back cover might prevent your phone from properly venting and result in heating problems.
- Playing games or using your phone excessively while it's charging is not advised.
- When charging the Samsung Galaxy S24 smartphone, make sure to always use the original charger.
- The main cause of a phone overheating is prolonged gaming. It is a widespread problem with nearly all smartphones.
- Installing unsupported apps and games on your phone is not advised. Many times, it results in overheating.
- Update all of your apps regularly and keep your phone up to date.
- Keep your phone's storage from ever filling up. Your phone might become sluggish and have heating problems as a result.
- Sometimes, even heating problems can arise as a result of your home's high temperature.
- Get your app from the Google Play Store at all times.
- Occasionally, internet-downloaded apps may result in temperature problems.
- The Samsung Galaxy S24 smartphone overheating issue is also primarily caused by an unhealthy and/or outdated battery.

Poor Battery Life

The procedures listed below can be used if the battery on your Samsung Galaxy S24 is depleting quickly. **You can determine the root of the problem on your smartphone by doing the procedures listed below.**

Solution

- When not in use, turn the GPS off at all times.
- Uninstall any installed apps, such as Phone Cleaner. These background-running apps drain the battery on your phone.
- Apps should only ever be downloaded from the Play Store. These apps might include malware that causes problems with your phone's battery draining by operating in the background.
- Try to use your phone in general settings at all times. Poor battery life may be caused by using your Samsung Galaxy S24 device in custom settings, which you should avoid doing.
- Try getting a new battery for your phone if you notice a sharp drop in its battery life.
- Using the Samsung Galaxy S24 with its screen brightness set too high could quickly drain its battery.
- Your battery draining quickly should also be attributed to the amount of games you play.
- Check to see if installing any apps on your phone has affected your battery life.
- Uninstall any apps you may have installed if they make promises to increase your phone's battery backup.
- Long periods spent in power-saving mode on your phone also quickly drain the battery.
- Try doing a factory reset on your Samsung Galaxy S24 if the battery problem persists after completing the aforementioned steps.

A Laggy or Sluggish User Interface on your Samsung Galaxy S24

Does your phone's user interface seem sluggish and lag when you use it? If so, this is your device's comprehensive solution. Before implementing the instructions on your phone, please carefully read them through.

Solution

- Uninstall any antivirus or trash removal apps that you may be using on your phone.

- Make sure to unroot your device if you have rooted it because rooting can occasionally lead to problems.
- Verify that there is still enough space on your internal phone storage. Your Samsung Galaxy S24 phone will return to normal if you make some space available if it is nearing its storage limit.
- Connect your phone to a laptop or PC, and then use Quick Heal or another reliable antivirus program to scan it. Your phone's virus will be eliminated.
- Occasionally, a slow internet connection may cause you to experience lag and sluggishness.
- If the issue persists after completing the aforementioned steps, consider factory resetting your phone.
- Your phone will most likely operate much more quickly after a factory reset than it did before.
- Uninstall any apps that you find to be unnecessary.
- Occasionally, utilizing a personalized theme on your phone could cause it to operate slowly.
- This issue may arise if you installed a third-party launcher on your Samsung Galaxy S24 recently. You can remove it and use the original theme again.
- Try giving your device a simple reboot to see if that resolves the problem.
- Verify that the most recent Android version is installed on your phone. If not, update to the most recent operating system for your phone.

Camera Issues on Samsung Galaxy S24

Samsung's new Galaxy S24 phone has been experiencing camera problems. The random shutdown of the phone's camera is happening, though it's unclear why. To fix it, just follow the steps listed below.

Solution

- This problem is brought on by an Android OS bug. Before you can fix it, you must wait for an official update from Samsung!
- Simply go back to the original camera settings if you're experiencing issues.
- Activate Image Stabilization on your camera to maximize its performance.
- If the issue persists, try clearing the cache of the camera app and opening it once more.
- To get better-quality images, you can activate the HD option within the camera application.
- If you have adjusted the Camera Settings, go back to the original settings and see if the issue has been resolved.

- Take off the screen protector from your phone and see if that fixes the problem.
- To resolve blurry photo issues, you should also clean the lens on your Samsung Galaxy S24 camera.

Samsung Galaxy S24 Phone shuts down unexpectedly

This is a fairly prevalent problem with Android phones. This problem causes your phone to abruptly shut off. Take into consideration the following actions if your Samsung Galaxy S24 smartphone is giving you trouble.

Solution

- First, make sure the battery in your Samsung Galaxy S24 is functioning properly.
- To make that happen, Enter *#*#4636#*#* into the phone dialer and press the dial.
- You can now see the information about the battery.
- Another possibility for the sudden phone shutdown could be a high temperature on your device.
- Avoid using heavy back covers as this can lead to poor ventilation and heating issues.
- Verify whether there is still space on your phone's internal storage. If not, this might be the cause of the sudden power outage.

Samsung Galaxy S24 Screen frozen or stuck

This issue is primarily caused by low RAM on your Android phone, and it can occur when playing games, performing tasks, or making calls. To fix this issue, follow the steps below.

Solution

- First, see if your smartphone has any Android updates. Update it right away if there's a new version available.
- You should force stop or uninstall any apps that you do not use from your phone.
- Try starting your Samsung Galaxy S24 in safe mode again and observe whether the issue resolves. If not, delete the offending app and perform a standard phone restart.
- When your phone's memory or storage is low, you might occasionally experience a frozen screen.
- If this problem arises when utilizing an app, then:
  Select **Apps > View All Apps**. Choose the app that is giving you trouble, and then delete its cache.

- Factory resetting your Samsung Galaxy S24 smartphone is the final step. All of your issues might be resolved by it.

Apps Opening Slow on the Samsung Galaxy S24

You have probably noticed a lot of times how slowly some apps open. This problem will arise on all phones. **If your phone experiences this problem, just take the easy steps listed below.**

Solution

- First, make sure there is adequate space on your phone's internal storage. If not, check after deleting a few trash files.
- This problem frequently results from your phone's incorrect RAM management. The RAM Booster App is useful in that situation. It will benefit you in terms of your device's overall performance.
- Verify whether your device has any mod games or apps installed. If it has been installed, immediately remove it from the Samsung Galaxy S24 device.
- Should the issue arise across all applications, you will need to restart and inspect your phone. This increases the likelihood of success.
- Make use of the App's lite edition. It will shorten the time it takes for an app to open and use less RAM.
- Should this problem persist, it would be best to factory reset your phone.

Apps Crash Suddenly

An app or game that unexpectedly closes when you open it is a common issue that can be resolved by following the instructions provided below.

Solution

- To start, locate the app that's giving you trouble by going to **Settings > Apps**. Choose the app and delete the information.
- Verify that there is at least 1 GB of storage remaining in your phone's internal storage.
- Reinstall the app after uninstalling the problematic one. It'll resolve the crash issue with the app.
- Ensure that the app is updated to the most recent version.
- Make sure to turn off Power Saving Mode and Safe Mode if you have them activated.
- Finally, use an antivirus app to scan your device.

Fingerprint Scanner problem

An additional degree of security is offered by the fingerprint scanner feature on the Samsung Galaxy S24. On the other hand, a few users have mentioned that their devices' fingerprint scanners are broken. We will demonstrate the solution in this section.

Solution

- Cleaning the sensor with a gentle cloth or tissue is one approach that might work.
- Take out the registered fingerprint and reapply for a fresh one.
- Another option is to try updating the software on your Samsung Galaxy S24 device. New updates might include fixes for any problems you're having with the fingerprint sensor.
- Reinstalling the firmware linked to your device's biometric features is an additional choice that, in certain cases, can assist in resolving fingerprint sensor-related problems.
- In the end, to determine and resolve any particular issues you might be experiencing with the fingerprint sensor on your device, you might need to speak with Samsung customer service.

Cellular network issue

We frequently experience problems with cellular networks on practically all smartphones. Try the following steps if your phone network is fluctuating or if you are not receiving a good signal.

Solutions

- Remove the SIM card and replace it with the original one from your Samsung Galaxy S24 device.
- If the issue persists, activate Airplane Mode, and then turn it off again after a short while.
- You might attempt to reset your network settings.
- Obstacles that stand in the way of your phone and the cell tower can frequently cause this problem.
- Try restarting your phone to see if the issue has been fixed.
- Verify whether a recently installed app is the cause of your network problems.

The display is cracked and the touch not working. Follow the instructions below if the display on your Samsung Galaxy S24 is broken and you want to access the data.

Solution

- You can link your Samsung Galaxy S24 to your PC or laptop with a USB cable. You can quickly access all of your data by doing this.
- Take out and re-insert any micro SD cards if you have data stored on them. See if that resolves the problem.
- One possible cause of the issue could be the screen sensor failing. Examine it and take the necessary measures.
- You can use an OTG cable to use any apps on your phone. Link your wireless mouse and keyboard. You can use your phone just like a PC in this way.

Conclusion

The capabilities of a smartphone are redefined by the Samsung Galaxy S24 series. The Galaxy S24 series elevates your mobile experience with its cutting-edge AI improvements. Now, you can search, message, and make calls in entirely new ways that cut through barriers related to time, language, and productivity. With the amazing camera setup found on the Galaxy S24 smartphone series, your photos will appear even better than before. Modern mobile camera setups are a hallmark of the Samsung Galaxy S series, and the new Galaxy S24 series lives up to expectations.

You can anticipate top-notch lenses that turn your social media accounts into photographic works of art, and improved AI that takes exceptionally clear, bright photos even at night. Furthermore, with the significant performance improvements of the Galaxy S24 series, everything you do on your phone is elevated to a whole new level. You can now scroll, stream, and play games for even longer thanks to incredibly bright screens, potent processors, and long-lasting batteries. With its amazing QHD+ resolution and 2600 nits of brightness, the Galaxy S24 Ultra boasts the brightest phone screen to date. Everything you see is next level. Also, the stunning visuals, which feature in-the-moment shadows and reflections, guarantee lifelike gameplay.

Additionally, the adaptive refresh rate kicks in to deliver incredibly smooth gameplay as the tempo increases. With their lightning-fast touch response, the incredibly responsive screens are ideal for both gaming and scrolling, offering you unparalleled control and interaction at all times. This indeed is a masterpiece that you need to have in your hands! In summary, the journey through the pages of this book has revealed the Samsung Galaxy S24 series' fascinating evolution, highlighting its design innovations, technological advancements, and industry-changing effects. From the first iterations of the Galaxy S series to the most recent models, you are without doubt aware of Samsung's unwavering commitment to providing cutting-edge features, potent performance, and a flawless user experience.

INDEX

B

C

I

N

O

Q

R

S

U

Y

Z

Manufactured by Amazon.ca
Bolton, ON

38770110R00142